From Where Lions Speak

An Ordinary Mans Discovery Of
Peace, Fear And Belonging

Written By

Douglas P Andonian

Copyright © 2026 by

Douglas P Andonian

ALL RIGHTS RESERVED. NO part of this book may be reproduced or transmitted in any form by any means, electronic or mechanical, including photocopying and recording, or by any information storage and retrieval system, except as may be expressly permitted in writing from the author.

ISBN

Paperback: 978-1-971045-17-7

Hardcover: 978-1-971045-18-4

Published by:
Pine Book Writing
www.PineBookWriting.com
R-10225 Yonge St Suite #250, Richmond Hill, ON L4C 3B2, Canada.

Printed in the United States of America

Acknowledgment

My intent was to choose individuals to recognize and thank for their guidance and influence throughout my life. The issue became the overwhelming number of people who, in a myriad of ways, played a significant role in helping to shape all aspects of my life. I've decided to choose a somewhat unorthodox approach to recognizing all of you. I trust you'll know who you are.

To parents who provided security, guidance, stability, and structure.

To a lady whose support early on will forever be appreciated and never forgotten. Thank You

To all who took the time to teach me. I can appreciate the struggle that must have been.

To all who took their precious time to help me in any way, at any time, whenever I asked.

To anyone who unselfishly offered their counsel to me when and if the need arose.

To all who politely suffered through a story I told, whether you wanted to hear it or not. You should think twice about agreeing to do it again.

To anyone who has been foolish enough to think they could assist with enhancing my golf game. Nice try!

To all who put a smile on my face or gave me a reason to laugh.

To anyone who encouraged me along the way.

Thank you all for your participation in the enrichment of my life.

Doug

Table of Contents

Chapter 1: In The Beginning 1

Chapter 2: The Process 12

Chapter 3: The Effect 27

Chapter 4: Peace 40

Chapter 5: Staying Awake 54

Chapter 6: On Being Witness 64

Chapter 7: Images 79

Chapter 8: Native People 96

Chapter 9: Observations 110

Chapter 10: In Conclusion 125

Chapter 1:
In The Beginning

I've agonized a great deal deciding how to commence this writing. At first, I thought it best to provide a detailed chronology of my childhood. I then decided, so as not to bore you with what I'm sure would put you to sleep, I would simply provide a short list, a profile of sorts, an outline, a window into the composition of an ordinary guy named Doug.

May, 1949, born in Massachusetts to first-generation American-born parents of Armenian descent. Truly great people, certainly not of means.

I think from birth, a patently observant child, and one who proved to be annoyingly curious. Growing up, a willing participant in mostly unorganized sporting activities, not athletically gifted, slow, and not very strong. I did, however, possess an extremely gifted eye for anything born of artistic design. Had my gifted eye been looked upon as an athletic attribute, I would have been in great demand and never defeated. Patience was never a virtue. I grew to better understand it as the years have gone by, and came to realize it can serve you well. Funny thing, I discovered it in a place I never would have imagined. Stay tuned.

Chapter 1: In The Beginning

Something I came to be very proud of was never being outworked by anyone I grew up with or would come to know. I worked extremely hard at anything that interested me and gave no effort to things I saw as mundane or not worthy of consideration. Truth is, it holds true today and can be traced directly back to the early days when I was delivering newspapers, mowing people's lawns in the summer, shoveling snow from driveways through the winter, and through high school working at my father's service station seven or eight hours a day after school and ten to twelve a day during summer vacation from classes. Sometimes it wasn't easy working with him every day. He expected a great deal from me and tolerated no less than the best I could give to the job at hand. Patience with me was never his strong suit. He held the belief that the process of learning is best achieved by observation, questioning, and ultimately doing. It was the process that was important in his mind. If you don't think that much time together initiated a great deal of verbal confrontation, think again, my friends. Sometimes, we were together too long and or too often. At times, our relationship seemed somewhat competitive. I guess the more I learned, the stronger my independence grew. It could be that it's just a natural transition. At this point, it's of no significance. I don't mean to leave anyone with the impression he was a monster; he certainly was not. He was a good teacher and, in the end, wanted only the best for me. Putting aside all the daily ups and downs, arguments and disagreements, we always maintained an unspoken degree of mutual respect for each other. I would surrender all in my life to have him and those long days at the shop back again. I developed a successful business in my early twenties and have the work ethic inspired by my father to thank. I think it became an integral part of the mold from which my future was derived.

Those who knew me best would often say they saw creative talent within me. I never paid any attention until later in life. Admittedly, a huge mistake, I should have listened. Through high school, teachers and guidance counselors encouraged me to attend college and, upon graduation, pursue a career in the field of creative writing. Most said they saw unique composition skills within me. I now wonder where that may have led had I listened.

In recent times, following retirement, I've produced two documentary films. Both speak to matters related to the Second World War. Each required scripts to be written, countless presentations to prepare, and permits to apply for. The production aspect for each project was quite involved and extremely time-consuming. Interestingly, the very thing I was encouraged to pursue but had rejected, I found myself having to engage in some forty years after the fact. Neither of the productions realized commercial success, and I must admit I gave that aspect of the process little to no effort. They were born from passion and selfishness. However,

Chapter 1: In The Beginning

both were well accepted and lauded by the audiences they drew at the festivals that screened them. One was the recipient of a director's choice award, of which I'm quite proud, not having had any prior filmmaking experience. The motivation to produce both was purely selfish and remains a story unto itself. Possibly, someday I'll tell that story in another writing. The entire process involved in their making is deserving of full disclosure. I've also come to appreciate a great deal of satisfaction from the results of the photography I discovered a passion for late in my life. You'll share a glimpse of that throughout this book.

Taking a step back, this is where the story really begins. My mother's younger brother, Harry, maintained a yearly subscription to National Geographic magazine. At this time, I was five or six years old, and the curiosity aspect of my personality was just taking root. In the 1950s, the magazine seemed to quite often feature writings and photographs with a focus on Southern and Eastern Africa. I believe because at the time, that unique part of the globe and the cultures that existed within it were so exotic and beyond the reach and imagination of the greater world population. It seemed to be a forgotten place. As young as I was, I was fascinated by what I saw in those magazines. These many years later, I can now fess up to having stolen time with Harry's National Geographic collection. Looking through them and having difficulty believing there could be places inhabited by such an abundance of amazing wildlife was an adventure in itself. When I was finished navigating my way through them and with the skill of a surgeon, I neatly returned them to their original position within his library of reading material. Because I was afraid to do so, I never sought permission to look at those magazines. I'm not sure my life would have been worth two cents had I been caught removing them from their well-organized stacks. Harry was attending college during this time and did not possess a great sense of humor. Life for him was fast becoming a serious thing, and any intrusion into Harry's world could have proven as dangerous as an encounter with predator cats.

This is about the time I began telling my parents, and anyone else who would listen, that someday I would go to Africa to see for real what I saw in those publications. African wildlife, free to roam unencumbered across a magnificent landscape deeded to them by their Maker. I wanted to see it, smell it, and learn firsthand about the seriousness of where I would be. My parents were convinced they had produced a very strange child. I recall my father looking directly into the center of my eyes, wanting to know why taking me to the zoo wasn't enough. My response to the question was a six-year-old's profound rebuke of the notion, a zoo could be a legitimate substitute for the reality of experiencing an untouched Africa. I'm convinced both he and my mother, or anyone else for that matter, could never understand. After all, everything there can hurt you. Why would

Chapter 1: In The Beginning

anyone ever consider accepting the risks involved? At the time and to that end, maybe my innocence was on display.

As years passed, the insatiable desire I possessed to experience the African bush grew and established permanent residence in the forefront of my spirited young mind. Academically, through the years, I certainly was never close to challenging genius status. I was not a reader, I was never going to be the one who would calculate that which was necessary to get to the moon, and I never understood why anyone should care about ancient history. For me, it was all Africa all the time, then and forever.

Anything one wants to do or a place anyone desires to see requires money and time. I didn't come from a place that provided either. The prospect of ever seeing anyplace beyond Cape Cod was a mere fantasy. Not a minute went by that the thought of lions and leopards didn't provide the incentive I needed to challenge the day. I don't consider that to have been odd. At some point in time, we all need something in our lives to strive for. Something that provides purpose and meaning to life. Early in mine, I was fortunate to have found that something.

A great deal of the time I spent with my father at the service station, I must admit, proved extremely valuable. When the seemingly nonstop activity would temporarily subside, an opportunity arose for us to relax for a short time and talk. Our conversations covered a myriad of topics. Politics, cars, people, sports, and some things I'd rather not mention. One topic in particular always had to do with the current status of the Red Sox, being that many of the players were customers we saw regularly at the station. Quite a few lived in the city where the shop was located. It was great. Game tickets were available to us anytime the team was home, and I took advantage of that as often as I could. My summertime dates were given no choice but to sit quietly under the lights through nine innings of Red Sox baseball at Fenway Park. I hope they appreciated the opportunity.

What I'm about to relate to you is what has ultimately had the most profound effect on me to this point in my life. A lesson my father unknowingly taught me and proved to serve me well at a later date.

Every so often, he would tell me how one day he would like to return to the Ardennes Forest in Belgium, where he and his tank battalion had been assigned for a time during the Second World War. Putting aside the purpose for his being there, he came to embrace the serenity and beauty of the landscape as well as the appreciation of the people for our military being present. I visited the Ardennes myself and can attest to his reasons for wanting to return to see it at peace. I recall, every so often he would suggest to my mother, they take a trip to Belgium so she could see and understand how and why

Chapter 1: In The Beginning

it inspired him. The purpose was never to discuss activities of the time he was there; it was simply to visit a place, one last time, that occupied a significantly special part of his heart and mind. He would express his frustration to me when she would repeatedly refuse to say yes to allocating two weeks of her life to afford him the opportunity to once again embrace the tranquility he felt being there. Again, putting aside circumstances at the time. It was important to him, and it would infuriate me knowing my mother would repeatedly refuse the simple request he made. I remember telling her each time he approached the subject and she refused to consider the suggestion, just how unfair it was of her. I tried to impress upon her the truth that he never intended to school her regarding the war. The journey was to show her from where his peace had been found. I think we all need to find our peace. To that end, the journey never came to be and proved so very wrong. At one point, I recall asking him why he continually insisted on giving her the opportunity to say no. I told him, being married to her for forty years should have taught him that, given the chance to say no, she would. He then asked me how I'd handle the situation. I told him he simply needed to make the arrangements, present the travel documents to her, and point out the dates she needed to have free. I told him not to make it any more complicated than that. I tried to impress upon him, she didn't need to be given a choice. His response was priceless. He hoped to live long enough to see me married and succeed in pulling off a stunt like that. He saw me married, but unfortunately, he did not survive to experience my skillful execution of what I had suggested to him.

VINNIN SQUARE SHELL

In August 1972, an opportunity arose for me to lease a service station about eight to ten miles from my father's location. He and I discussed my leaving his shop to take advantage of that opportunity and agreed I should do it, that he was considering retirement in a couple of years. I was twenty-three years old at the time and confident I could succeed on my own. I successfully executed that lease for four or five years and soon after found myself in Northern California working for a Chevrolet Oldsmobile dealer, having a possible opportunity to buy into an ownership position. As time went on, that opportunity faded away, and I returned east. The next

Chapter 1: In The Beginning

couple of years were uneventful, and I was not sure what to do. I was getting bored and didn't think it was best for my father to get any more relaxed than he was. I suggested to him, we look for a property to buy and establish another shop. He agreed, and so the search began. It didn't take but a few short months, we came across a suitable property in a great location, made an offer that was accepted, and set up shop. That location was home for the next twenty-five years. Not long after establishing the new business, I had the good fortune to meet a great lady who would ultimately become my future wife. We dated and, a few years later, decided to marry. She brought a son and two daughters along. All three are highly intelligent with a great sense of humor and an admirable work ethic. My wife had become casually aware of my hope to someday see Africa, but there wasn't a lot of talk or discussion about it. It was never dwelt upon. She was never aware or knew to what degree that fire burned within me.

Following my father's passing in November 1996, I left the house one morning at five o'clock as I always did, stopped to get my coffee and a bagel, and continued to the shop. I went into my office, turned on the TV to watch the news, and started to think about my father. He was now deceased, and I was in the midst of dealing with the onset of my mother's Alzheimer's disease. At that point in time, the reality was, neither of them were going anywhere. The opportunity to return to Belgium was gone forever. It was then, I realized the fragility of life and the ridiculousness of thinking, I'll see Africa someday. At that moment, there just didn't appear to be any advantage to waiting. The time had come. My Mother was receiving the professional care she needed, I was comfortable the business was in capable hands, and I found myself with the means and was simply going to allocate the time. Just one trip. I was sure that would satisfy me and extinguish the fire that burned within.

Later that morning, I turned my computer on and began a search for travel agents whose expertise was designing African safaris. I came across an interesting website belonging to an agent in Santa Barbara, California, whose specialty was putting together safari itineraries. I called, spoke to the owner of the agency, and was subsequently turned over to a safari designer who was originally from South Africa. Leora was young, energetic, well-travelled, and proved to know the landscape well. The jackpot had been struck. It was now time for me to teach a deceased man how it's done, and so I did just that.

Chapter 2: The Process

Contact with the travel agent began in mid-March, 1997. My original intent was to make this journey with just my wife. I began to think better of that and decided to include her two girls, Tracy and Nichole. Both had graduated from college, and neither was married. It was the right time to gift the experience to them, and would offer their mother a degree of added comfort. I knew her son would have no desire to see or spend one minute in the African bush; it just wasn't his kind of place. I had not said a word to anyone regarding the planning of this trip. Arrangements were being made allowing for sixteen days, a year from the time the itinerary was finalized. Everyone's life-altering adventure would take place in April, 1998. The fun aspect of this for me was not letting on that it was about to happen.

For four to six weeks, calls and emails travelled back and forth between me and Leora. She asked important questions with a focus on specific interests we might have. I told her photography would most likely dominate the day-to-day activity; however, I wanted everyone to experience an all-encompassing journey. It was important to me that we come away learning behavioral aspects of the wildlife, the diversity of the landscapes, and an appreciation of the cultures we would encounter. With those goals in mind, she suggested we stay at four safari camps, two in each of two countries, Botswana and Namibia. Following my review of the specific locations she thought would be best, we agreed, discussed a few remaining details, and having done that, secured the itinerary.

When the travel documents had been prepared and I had paid for everything, I asked Leora to forward the package to my office. When they arrived, I reviewed them and brought them home that evening after work. I remember walking into the house to find my wife preparing dinner. I then made a colossal mistake. I told Judy to call the girls and have them come to the house that evening. She asked why, and I told her I needed to talk to everyone. With a somewhat troubled expression on her face, she once again asked for what reason. I answered her question, telling her she'd find out when the girls arrived. Another blunder. Both girls appeared about the same time, and I proceeded to ask everyone to take a seat around the kitchen table. For a short time, the atmosphere was a bit tense. I'm sure they were all convinced I was going to inform them of some incurable medical issue that had befallen me. A totally wrong approach, to say the least.

I began by telling them it would be necessary for us all to have 16 specific days available in April, beginning one year from the day of this evening's discussion. I think before asking why, I observed everyone taking a deep breath. I wanted to believe it was due to their realizing all was fine with me. I then informed everyone that we would be away for those sixteen days. Of course, the next logical question was where. As soon as I uttered the word Africa, the girls were packed and ready to go. I can't remember ever seeing them as excited as they were that night. My wife, without a moment's hesitation, said she was not coming with us. When questioned about her refusal to join us, she responded by telling me she had no interest in seeing anything in any part of Africa and followed that with a question as to where we were going to sleep. As soon as I informed her we would sleep in the comfort of a canvas tent, she responded by telling me and the girls to enjoy ourselves. At that moment, I would have given anything to have my father seated at that table. This would have been the perfect opportunity to take him to school.

I knew Judy would react, as she did, but I had prepared for it. Throughout the remainder of the discussion and the never-ending questions from the girls, I purposely avoided including my wife in any of it. It was so interesting watching her stew, wanting so badly to ask questions and be involved in the conversation. The girls couldn't seem to understand how or why I seemed to have no problem with their mother's refusal to make the trip. They didn't know that I knew she ultimately would. They knew nothing of my plan. I knew she needed time; it was the sole reason we wouldn't embark on the journey for another year. The girls left that night very excited. I'm sure they were somewhat perplexed as to why we were not going to leave on the trip for another year. It would have proven to be another mistake to make them aware of why that needed to be.

The list of things we needed to do in preparation seemed to grow exponentially. Passports needed to be valid and in order; a visit to the travel clinic for required inoculations had to be scheduled, and proper clothing was necessary. Of great importance was functioning camera gear, and in addition, a never-ending catalog of incidental items. Fortunately, time was on our side. As the clock began ticking, every so often, when I would arrive home from work, Judy would ask a question about some aspect of the trip. The queries she had were about things such as food. What would we be eating? She was horrified at the thought, it might consist of the very game we saw during the day. Having researched such things, I assured her it would not. The camps would prepare, for us, what we were accustomed to. She then asked about laundry. I informed her, laundry would be done for us daily. I asked why such things concerned her, having already been informed she wasn't coming with us. Crickets. One question she had presented an opportunity for me to visually take her to Africa, right around the corner from our home. Let me explain: she was unaware of the physical environment we would be in. Not sure if it consisted of jungle or some other landscape. In an effort to answer the question, I suggested we take a drive after dinner. I drove her a short distance from the house to a local farm she had seen a

Chapter 2: The Process

thousand times. I pointed to the vast acreage of grassland, numerous islands of trees, and a large pond that was on the property. That particular evening, there were also cows wandering about. I told her, for the most part, this is what she would see. There was no verbal response; however, the visual seed had been planted. I sensed the plan was working. We returned home from our domestic safari that evening, and without any further discussion of the upcoming trip, we retired to bed.

As the months rolled by, the to-do list was becoming shorter. Passports were up to date, the appointment with the travel clinic had been made, and the anticipation had grown to a level I never could have imagined. You might have thought I was taking ten-year-old kids to Disneyland. To be honest, me included.

One Friday evening, I think in August or September, Judy asked what my plans were for Saturday. I told her, in the morning, I was going to take the girls to a nearby retail outfitter to find a couple of sets of clothes for the trip. She got somewhat excited and told me she would come with us since she had nothing else planned. Just to be difficult and keep the game alive, I casually told her there was no need for her to come. She was not about to be told she couldn't come to assist the girls in making their selections. I did well not to exacerbate that situation. I should mention she found a couple of safari outfits for herself. When I asked why she had chosen to buy safari clothing she wasn't going to need, she told me they would be comfortable around the house and while working in the yard. Now I knew she was about to melt. Christmas was fast approaching, and Judy asked what I intended to do for the girls. I told her I had been informed that Nichole had a functioning camera body, but her two lenses were not reliable. Tracy had a functioning lens, but her camera body was working intermittently. That made Christmas easy and moderately expensive.

January arrived, and one night early in the month, while having dinner, my wife informed me that although she had no desire to experience Africa, she was of the opinion the girls would enjoy it to a greater extent and feel somewhat more comfortable if she were with us. I had no cause to doubt the girls had influenced their mother's decision to accompany us. I told her, that explained the book titled Namibia, that I saw on her nightstand. She didn't know I had seen it. She then asked if it was too late to add her to the group. If only to be difficult, I told her I'd have to look into it. She had no idea her arrangements were already in place, nor did the girls. Everything was in order. Oh, where was my father? The stunt he referred to had succeeded. I admit I took a somewhat different approach by way of allowing Judy to think it was her decision to make the trip, but so what? In the end, it all came to fruition. I never had a doubt it would.

Chapter 2: The Process

February arrived, and it was time to visit the travel clinic. They asked what countries we would be traveling to, then went directly to the CDC manual to administer the proper shots and dispense the oral medications we would need. They consisted of protection from such things as hepatitis A, typhoid, polio, malaria, and tetanus-diphtheria. There may have been others. I can't remember. We were poked in the arm so many times, had we taken a drink of water, we would have leaked enough to be rivaled only by the outdoor fountain at a prominent Las Vegas hotel. Better safe than sorry, I guess. Now it was just a matter of waiting for April to arrive. It would prove to be the most agonizing couple of months I can remember. At no other time in my life can I recall being as excited and totally focused on what was about to take place. At forty-seven years old, I was about to have the experience I had dreamt about and longed for all my life. The impossible was finally going to become a reality.

I had arranged for a sitter to stay at the house to take care of our two Labrador Retrievers. I couldn't bring myself to kennel them. Judy wouldn't have any part of that either. Early, the morning of April 10th, 1998, the limousine I had arranged pulled into the driveway to pick us up, and off we went to catch our flight from Boston to New York. We had a short wait before boarding a grueling sixteen-and-a-half-hour nonstop flight to Johannesburg, South Africa. We all tried to sleep during the flight, but I guess the excitement was too great to permit that to happen. I'm sure every so often, there were short naps enjoyed. We were taken good care of while in the air. The meals were fine, the available entertainment was a welcome component, and the flight crew could not have been any more accommodating.

During a flight of that duration, one certainly has a great deal of time to think. In my case, I began to question how I might handle the possibility of having to come to grips with discovering Africa was just a big zoo. What would I do after waiting so long, finally being in a position to realize what had been an impossible dream, not to mention the enormous amount of money involved? Nothing in recent memory frightened me more. The thought of that becoming a reality came close to being incentive enough to push the call button and request oxygen. I think the length of the flight simply provided too much time to contemplate a potentially negative experience. When all was said and done, it was anything but that.

Upon arrival in Johannesburg, we were met and transferred to a hotel just outside the airport. We stayed the night and in the morning were flown to Botswana, where we would stay at two camps for the next seven days.

The single-engine bush flights we took to reach the camps and the dirt airstrips we took off from and subsequently landed on were certainly nothing short of an adventure. There were times it was

Chapter 2: The Process

necessary to remind yourself where you were and what you had signed up for.

The daily routine at the camp consisted of early morning coffee, followed by a morning game viewing drive, either a mid-morning stop in the bush for a bite to eat or a return to camp for breakfast, a continuation of your game drive, and a return to camp for lunch. Because not much in the way of wildlife activity exists during midday, everyone relaxes either at their tent to catch a short nap or at the main lounge area to read or talk to other guests. You quickly come to embrace the midday rest. Riding in the safari vehicle over rough terrain can certainly become a bit uncomfortable. The break is generally a welcome one. Late in the afternoon, coffee, cold drinks, and sweets are offered prior to a late afternoon game drive and a stop in the bush to enjoy drinks, hors d'oeuvres, and to experience magnificent sunsets. Darkness brought about a return to camp for dinner. The days are never void of activity.

The first camp we stayed at was in the Okavango Delta on the Moremi Wildlife Reserve. When we landed, we were met by our guide and driven by Land Rover to the camp. Upon arrival, the entire staff greeted us with arms waving, the widest smiles I've ever seen, moist hand towels, and cold drinks. Unquestionably first class. We were greeted by management, welcomed, and advised as to what, and what not to do during our stay. Such things as no walking around camp or anywhere else unaccompanied after sundown, and a few other things that I don't even remember.

Next was a walk to our tents for the purpose of familiarizing us with things such as where to leave the laundry, and again, that which I can't remember. One thing they seemed insistent upon. There was a marine air horn sitting on a nightstand next to the bed. They were a fixture in each tent. I was instructed to only use it during a medical emergency. I remember asking the girl assigned to our tour, "You're telling me if one night a lion tries to penetrate this tent, I can't blow this horn off for help?" My thought was, an incident of that nature would, in effect, create a medical emergency. Her response was "please don't". Twenty-some odd years later, and I still have no idea what I was supposed to do had we been confronted with that situation.

This orientation proved to be the norm at all camps at which we stayed. Judy and the girls were enthralled with the accommodations of their tents. That comforted me a great deal. Both camps in Botswana were well beyond expectations and quickly dispelled any and all negative thoughts I may have had on the plane. The day and night game drives, gourmet meals, remote locations, and the complexity of the environment we were in were overwhelming. This was shaping up to be well worth the years of waiting. It was the first time in my life that I was convinced I belonged somewhere.

The second camp in Botswana was an equally positive adventure. Wildlife sightings were nonstop, the staff was very attentive, the food could not have been better, and the river environment surrounding the camp was breathtaking. Kudos to the guide and tracker. They could not have been any more knowledgeable and interesting to converse with.

Northern Namibia proved to be a totally different environment. The region we visited in the north was mountainous and stunningly beautiful. The first camp we stayed at was not particularly exciting. I actually found it to be somewhat disappointing. The accommodation was cottage-type as opposed to canvas tents. It was located just outside Etosha National Park. I never quite understood; we were never asked if we'd like to visit the park. I found that to be a bit strange.

Three nights... we were there for three nights and just couldn't find a way to like the place. Although there were wildlife sightings, it simply was not the Africa we experienced during the prior week.

Chapter 2: The Process

Our final four nights were magnificent. We were in the Omboroko mountains of Namibia at a cheetah sanctuary and rehabilitation facility.

When making the arrangements for the trip a year earlier, I insisted we include this particular camp as part of the itinerary, having seen it featured in a documentary on one of the television nature channels I frequently watched. It piqued my interest, and I saw no reason not to see it while there. The young couple who owned and operated the camp could house guests in ten cottages that had been constructed on the property. Revenue generated from people coming to stay and observe the work being done is what helped finance the rehab effort. The cottages were quite comfortable and were located bordering a sprawling grass lawn and in close proximity to a comfortable thatched roof dining deck. The couple's home was in a secluded area on the property, as well as a building that served as a veterinary facility. When an injured animal, or one needing medical attention for any reason, was brought in and the local vet was called to administer care, most he or she needed in the way of equipment and a proper place to work was available on site. Large fenced enclosures were constructed to provide the cheetah, being attended to and rehabbed, an enormous area in which to roam, while at the same time remaining safe from any and all unwelcome outside influences. A truly unique operation and a priceless experience. It was well worth the visit. Judy and I would return the following year.

All that was left to do was return home. The reality of having to leave Africa was, without a doubt, the most depressing feeling one could ever have. In my case, maybe, just maybe, once would never prove to be enough. I'll admit, I already knew it wouldn't.

Chapter 2: The Process

The experience of seeing all those predator cats, elephants, zebras, giraffes, and all other species roaming freely was beyond my wildest imagination. Judy, Tracy, and Nichole were awestruck every minute of every day we were there. For me, it was well beyond being awestruck.

Chapter 3:
The Effect

The flight home was long and tiring. I will admit I took advantage of the opportunity to sleep a little on the plane. I think earlier I mentioned not usually doing that when I fly. No doubt decompression from all the excitement of two weeks living a dream brought that about.

When we arrived home, we departed the limousine, carried all the bags into the house, and were greeted by the dogs. They made us feel they were happy to see us. I wanted to believe that was the case, but I couldn't be sure. Anyway, all seemed to be in order. The girls left soon after to catch the photo shop before it closed, anxious to drop off their film for processing. I waited until the following day to do the same. I did find it odd that, having brought forty-two rolls of film with me, I had only shot twenty-three of the forty-two. Thinking about that made me realize just how disciplined I had been with the camera. I had no prior experience with photo equipment and prayed every day, following the trip, that I would prove to have been a photographic prodigy. The discipline aspect had to do with my wanting to capture what I saw as the most unique wildlife compositions available to me. I soon discovered, accomplishing that required a great deal of patience and the willingness to sit in one

Chapter 3: The Effect

place for however long it took to acquire the desired pose. Prior to this adventure, patience had never occupied a place in my DNA. I learned in a hurry what patience was all about and just how important it was.

Well, it was back to the shop, and all that was a galaxy away from where I had just been. Reality had to establish itself immediately. Reflection would now have to wait until the drive home at the end of the day. After all, the shop is what provided the means necessary to realize the dream that often seemed unattainable. It required and deserved my utmost attention.

I was astounded by what I learned about myself while in Africa. Let's begin with the realization of fear. I think everyone experiences a degree of fear at some point in their life. I'm about to describe an encounter we had late one afternoon along the shoreline of a river while at the second camp in Botswana. I'll attempt to set the scene.

It was about four thirty in the afternoon, and we'd been driving in the Land Rover along the shoreline of the river I spoke of. Just a leisurely drive along a picturesque landscape before returning to camp. Our guide was driving, and his tracker was positioned in a seat mounted on the left front fender of the vehicle. He was secured within it only by way of a safety belt. Judy was sitting beside me, behind our guide and driver, KB. Tracy and Nichole were each in separate seats at the rear of the car. All was well. Unexpectedly, from the heavily treed area to our right, a herd of elephants emerged from the tree line on their way to the water with their little ones, apparently for an end-of-the-day drink, swim, and roll in the mud. We were approximately fifty or sixty yards away. We stopped, KB turned the car off, and we sat to observe the elephants' fun afternoon at the beach.

In short order, two adult bulls broke from the herd, turned toward us, and, having caught our scent and with trunks elevated, began a slow side-by-side walk in our direction. Just then, I heard Nichole nervously say, "Oh my God." I turned to see another herd emerge from the woods directly behind us. They too were on their way to the beach. This herd was somewhat closer. Among these elephants, only one turned toward us and began to slowly approach. In the meantime, the two bulls facing us broke into a slow trot, kicking up a little dust along the way and trumpeting a tune I'd never heard before. It scared the hell out of everyone in the car, so much so that the lone elephant approaching from the rear had long been forgotten. No doubt a serious warning. I think my blood pressure increased by a thousand points.

Chapter 3: The Effect

I experienced a true degree of fear when the tracker released his seat belt, crawled across the hood of the Rover, and fell into the front seat. KB and the tracker then engaged in some serious conversation in their native tongue. It was obvious that an effort was made to avoid injecting panic into the situation. Little did they know panic had already taken a seat in the car with us and quickly became a serious component of this terrifying event. The thought went through my mind, we could all become the lead story on the six o'clock news back home in Boston. Not my idea of the way to acquire fame.

I felt someone had to take control at this point, since no one had. I decided the only chance we had to avoid certain death was to back the car away from the approaching giants into the wooded area to our right. I could only hope they would then realize we were not a threat and make their way back to the herd. Forcefully, I suggested to KB that he start the car and immediately back into the trees behind us. At first, he paid little attention. Time was not on our side, and there was no chance for a negotiated settlement with these massive giants. Things were happening very fast. I soon lost what patience I had, but didn't want to demean KB or the tracker for their not being capable of making a decision. All I could do at this point was make it clear to him we had no choice. He finally agreed, took my advice, backed over a few fallen trees he didn't think he could, and the situation was summarily diffused.

The elephants turned away, collected the herd, and returned to the woods from where they had emerged. At this point, my heart rate returned to normal, Nichole stopped crying, Tracy sat fanning herself with a towel, and Judy thankfully stopped shaking. That's fear, my friends. True fear. Feeling the squeeze from both ends was not the least bit comforting. We were fortunate to live through the twenty-minute experience and, despite a few more close calls, we were able to enjoy the remainder of the trip. Having survived and from the comfort of home, I have to admit the encounter was very exciting, frighteningly so.

I tell you this story because I've come to learn that in one's lifetime, there are varying degrees of fear we all are certain to experience. To this point in my life, I had never felt heart-pounding fear like I did this day. If my heart was going to explode, this was the day and time it would have happened. If you had researched the definition of the word fear, it was more than likely all that would have appeared was an uncomplimentary photograph of me.

Following dinner, the day of the encounter, we were sitting around a blazing open fire, enjoying Amarula and wine by the light of oil lamps hanging from the trees and placed along the paths leading to where we were sitting. The sky was lit brightly by a vast concentration of stars. It was so quiet, and yet I knew so much activity was taking place around us. In Africa, darkness inspires the hunt, and most of those we had come to see were participants. Some were the hunted, others the hunters. For most, the African night is all about survival and the opportunity to experience the next sunrise.

While sitting around the fire, I began thinking how advantageous it was to have had the elephant confrontation as early in the trip as we did. It established the reality of where we were and dispelled the concern I had on the plane that Africa might prove to be nothing more than a large zoo. This place is for real. One needs to remain awake at all times while in the bush. Competing with stealth and instinct is impossible. I quickly realized, in this environment, we can't compete. One shouldn't tempt the strength, cunning, speed, and natural camouflage possessed by these native residents. Only a fool would challenge those attributes.

I'm going to break from the seriousness of all this and lighten things up a bit with a short story I think you'll enjoy. It puts a smile on my face every time I tell it to someone.

Our first night in Africa seemed to transport us to an unimaginable place. We were all tired by day's end. The travel was just excruciating. The girls retired to their tent, which was roughly thirty-five or forty yards from ours. I'm sure it didn't take long for them to fall asleep. Judy and I went to bed and, in a matter of minutes, began counting gazelles. At one point during the night, I felt myself being shaken. I opened my eyes and looked up to find Judy standing over me. I asked her what she was doing, at which point she placed her index finger over her mouth to signal me to be quiet, whereupon I looked at my watch; it was 2:15 am. How happy do you think I was at that moment? You guessed right if you said, not very.

I asked her what the need was to wake me. She replied by telling me she heard something outside the tent. I told her I didn't think that was unusual, as there was an abundance of wildlife that lived there, and most of their activity took place at night. I then calmly suggested she return to bed. If you knew this wonderful woman, you'd know how relentless she was when looking for an answer to something. I

Chapter 3: The Effect

tell you this because she would not give up having to know who had come to visit in the middle of the night. I simply couldn't convince her to return to bed. Most married guys I know would tell you, sometimes it's just easier to do what she asks. Works for me. Anyway, I got up, unzipped the mosquito netting, and proceeded to open the canvas to look outside.

To my amazement, there was a pride of lions, a couple of which were sniffing around the corners of the tent, others were in the tall grass across the path, and still more were making their way through camp. Without a moment's hesitation, I zipped the tent closed, turned to Judy, and quietly told her it was just a small herd of impala. Fortunately, she wasn't aware that impalas don't generally wander at night. I told her to go back to bed. She did, and in a matter of seconds, she was asleep.

I knew if I told her there were lions that close to where she was sleeping, the realization of my dream would have come to an abrupt end before it had a chance to begin. I wasn't proud of having lied to her, but knowing there was no bus to put her on in the morning, I had no choice. I must tell you, I was shaken by the sight of those lions, and as tired as I was, I never closed my eyes the rest of the night. To this day, some twenty-seven years later, Princess Judy still doesn't know they were lions. I'm thinking it might be wise to remove this page from her personal copy of the book.

After being in camp a few days, I began to experience a calm unlike anything I'd felt before. I was perfectly happy and willing to sit anywhere for any length of time to simply observe the goings on. It's interesting watching a male lion court a lioness for the sole purpose of mating. He's relentless in his pursuit of the lady he chose. It's all to do with her giving birth to his legacy and maintaining the existence and strength of the pride. It's priceless to observe a female baboon grooming her newborn and protecting it from all that might cause harm to it, not letting it wander beyond the extent of her reach. The more I observe the wildlife and the behavioral aspects of their lives, the greater my curiosity as to the purpose of this place and all its magnificent life forms. After all, they don't have jobs, they don't go to school, they don't shop for groceries, and they don't need homes or vehicles to transport them from one place to another. So what is their purpose for being? It can't simply be to provide a food source for each other. There must be one, quite possibly many. The reality is, they do need to participate in and accomplish everything on that list, not terribly unlike what's required of us, albeit in a somewhat different context. Still, the question remains: what is their purpose? I wonder sometimes if sitting comfortably, observing, and having time to think is something I shouldn't engage in too often while here. I should sit comfortably, observe, think, and ultimately simply embrace being one of the few to have had the good fortune to experience this jewel of a place as often as I have and will continue to do. I consider it to be the planet's largest diamond.

Making more of themselves is vital, and they're extremely successful at it. They do provide a food source for each other. Still, the question remains: what is the purpose of all this magic? I'm not a religious guy, a believer in God, but not to the extent he might like me to be. That said, the questions remain unanswered, but may prove to be one of many reasons I can't stop coming to paradise. I will say, one could see things here as being quite simple and easy to understand. To most, it may appear to be that way. I would argue that point. For what it does to me, there are no words.

Most of the time, it's so quiet and yet in an instant can explode into such raw violence. The explosion is generally isolated and occurs during the pursuit and takedown of prey. It's mesmerizing to witness a herd of buffalo running to escape the wrath of lions pursuing them, then stopping abruptly to watch as the hunters separate one from the herd and violently begin the process of ending its life. When it's over and the dust has settled, the lions begin their feast, and the buffalo herd simply moves on, calmly, with the relative assurance they can enjoy peace for a short while. Unlike our perception of conquest, the lions instinctively see no benefit to eliminating numbers beyond that which they need to satisfy today. They'll separate another in a few days. Scavengers will see to it that the land is kept clean. If, while here, you pay attention, you begin to realize what an amazing teaching place this is. You learn quickly, for most, survival within the wildlife community doesn't allow for a great deal of relaxation. Constant awareness is just one of many good qualities to possess.

One interesting observation I've made throughout my visits has to do with the native people. They talk to each other nonstop. I have no idea about what, who, or where, but it's nonstop. I wish I understood their native languages. I can only attribute their need to converse is rooted in not being concerned about matters such as material possessions. Cars, houses, lavish vacations. The things that seem to consume us. I've occasionally asked what they discuss and was told much of the talk centers on issues of family, situations that exist within the villages, wildlife concerns having to do with conservation, and matters of education for their young. I guess, things that really matter. Their minds seem to be clear and void of what can separate them from each other. I see and understand life here as more of a team sport. I'm not naive. I have no doubt that petty jealousies exist, and the desire to experience more in the way of material pursuit, on occasion, enters their minds. In the end, their faith, each other, and their precious environment rule most days. As I grow older, I'm becoming a fan of simplicity. I believe it has served my African friends well.

If attention is paid, one can learn a great deal from time in Africa. Through the years, coming here has inspired within me an appreciation for the coexistence among wildlife, the human influence, and the interaction between both. All seem to instinctively understand their place in the order of things. Infringement upon that order by either would most likely prove to be a grave error in judgment. If you desire to teach the virtue of respect to your children, bring them to the African bush. You might discover how very little would need to be said. Their observation skills would be sharpened, and I can assure you they would return home better, in all aspects of their lives, for having been to Africa.

I would prefer to die if told I could never again come to this magical place.

Chapter 4: Peace

It's been my long-held belief that most of us, at one time or another, have a desire to find peace in our lives. I have to think where we search for it, and to what degree we'd like to experience it is an individual thing. The pursuit of what might calm us can be difficult in that our lives are consumed with day-to-day challenges that monopolize a great deal of our time and effort. Trust me, I get it. I consider myself fortunate, having discovered my peace, albeit halfway around the world in an unexpected place at a time I wasn't even thinking about or looking for it. I guess in a true sense it found me. Africa, and the calming effect it immediately began to have on me, was a welcome surprise. I discovered, while there, I could shut out the world. I suddenly cared less about what might be happening anywhere else on the planet. Though everything there, large or small, could hurt me and, in an instant, bring about my demise, I was experiencing a calm I had never felt before. There certainly was no reason to spend time analyzing it. The key was to simply be thankful for having found it and embrace the good fortune to have done so.

Following our first trip to Africa, Judy and I were having dinner one evening and talking about a few different things, one of which involved a bit of reflection concerning an incident we encountered while on our first trip. To be specific, it had to do with a Black Mamba snake that was slithering alongside our Land Rover with its eye on a baby baboon sitting atop a termite mound just off our path. Baboons of all ages and sizes were sitting, some on the ground, others in the nearby trees, screaming bloody murder in an effort to warn the little one of the snake's approach. The baby seemed well aware of the hunter's presence but appeared unconcerned, continuing to snack on something it had picked up off the ground and carried to its perch atop the mound. The warning calls from family members and friends were deafening. As the Mamba began winding its way up and around the eight-foot-high mound, the little one would look periodically to monitor the snake's progress. I remember Nichole beginning to cry in anticipation of the possible violent end to the young baboon's life. Just as the highly venomous reptile had come within striking distance, ear-piercing screams from the troop positioned in the trees became near unbearable. My ears are still ringing from it. Realizing the time was now, the young baboon jumped from the mound and found its way to the safety of the elders. It was a heart-pounding thirty minutes, and I can assure you, not an event that put a smile on anyone's face. Occurrences of this type are commonplace in the bush; however, that fact makes them no less difficult to witness. The ladies were visibly shaken for the remainder of the day, and it left no question as to exactly where

Chapter 4: Peace

we were. Visual images taken from this place will most likely leave an indelible mark on your consciousness. Not all are pleasant.

At one point, after having discussed the Black Mamba incident, Judy stopped eating and quietly rested her fork on her plate. She looked at me and asked how soon I thought we could return to Africa. I knew then she had been overwhelmed and impressed by all she had seen, heard, and experienced while there. She, too, had been introduced to the concept and realization of having discovered peace. I don't know if she recognized it as such; however, I certainly did. There's no way you can mask it. I could tell by the tone and calm inflection in her speech when she spoke of anything to do with Africa. This place does that to you. You're wise not to question the peace you discover here; just be thankful you did. She had taken the bait, and I needed to strike while the iron was hot. I told her I wasn't sure when we could return, but the first order of business the next morning was to call Leora and begin the process of initiating another itinerary for the upcoming year. This time, there was no need to book a year ahead. Once more, I didn't tell Judy until the itinerary had been prepared. I didn't want to afford her enough time to cool off. I didn't feel she would, but one never knows.

We returned to Botswana and Namibia for another two weeks, again in April the following year. This time without the girls. Another fantastic adventure, very much the same but very different in many ways. Although the wildlife remains the same and only nature can seasonally alter the landscape, no two days are ever alike. For me, those factors are a vital component of what has created the need to return to a place that is unquestionably real, unpretentious, and serious. A place uncluttered by human insanity. The African bush represents all that is true. Don't believe me? Just ask Judy.

I was beginning to feel a wee bit possessive about the places we'd been, convincing myself I belonged there. I know now I did, and offer no apologies for the possessive attitude I've acquired. I often wonder each time I'm in the African bush how it is that, knowing I'm the weakest, least instinctive, and defenseless living thing, it's possible to allow myself the luxury of peace. It's a question I can't answer, and I'm even at peace with that.

Two years passed, and I made arrangements to return, this time with a desire to explore Zambia and Zimbabwe. Upon arrival in Zimbabwe, we stayed the first two nights at the luxurious Victoria Falls Hotel. An experience we could never have imagined. The accommodations were overwhelming, and the grounds equally so. The hotel provided an outdoor thatched dining area that created an ambiance that we had never before found ourselves within. Try to imagine the visual of mist and the sound of the falls as you dine outdoors on the grounds of what is one of the world's most famous hotels. Our brief stay provided an opportunity for us to see the

Chapter 4: Peace

world-famous Victoria Falls, gateway to the lower Zambezi River. From there, we began our two-week adventure on the river and one week in the South Luangwa region of Zambia. The guide we had on the crocodile and hippo-rich Zambezi was a former Zimbabwean park ranger. John set up camp for us within the Mana Pools National Park on the sandy bank of the massively wide river. Sunsets were amazingly stunning. What I remember most was the quiet. Not a sound to be heard. Only when a hippo rose from under the water and barked was there a break in the silence. Early in the morning, elephants would emerge from the forest, and through the light fog, we watched them raise their trunks and strip from the trees the leaves and small branches they fed upon. From seemingly nowhere, waterbuck would appear, and the baboons would begin foraging for breakfast. Only someone void of all senses could be unappreciative of all this.

One morning, John suggested we canoe down the river for a while. We agreed it would be a great couple of hours.

Judy occupied one canoe piloted by John, and I did the same with one of his porters piloting my canoe so I could capture some images as we made our way downstream. One thing you need to understand is the Zambezi River is croc-infested. They sun themselves on the sandbars and shoreline along the river, and when they sense a meal may be on the horizon, they quietly slide into the water, remain below the surface, and patiently wait for you or some other unsuspecting species to have the misfortune of somehow joining them in the water, where either will quickly become consummate fast food for them.

For purposes of this discussion and in full disclosure, at the time I was two hundred fifty pounds and not likely to survive a fall from an unstable canoe. There would have been enough of me available

Chapter 4: Peace

to keep a Nile crocodile fat and happy for a very long time. Upon completion of our expedition, we now had to navigate between two families of hippos in an effort to get to shore. As harrowing as all this may have been, I was at peace with myself and was quite willing to accept whatever risks there were. There may have been a degree of stupidity involved, but the peace I felt within far outweighed any other influence. It's strange how an environment you belong in can afford you peace, not found anywhere else, even when said environment is hostile.

It wouldn't be fair not to tell you Judy and I had a discussion that evening after having dinner and retiring to our tent for the night. The topic was the insanity of what we had agreed to do that day. You know, I was so beefy at that time, the crocodile that would have scored me had I fallen from the canoe would probably still be eating. That was twenty-five years ago. Frightening to say the least.

From Mana Pools, our next camp was on the Zambian side of the river downstream from where we had just been. The camp was fantastic and the staff equally so. Early one evening, we, and another couple who were guests at the camp, were taken by boat to a sandbar in the middle of the river. We were told to remain in the boat while the guide walked the length of the island to be sure we had no unwelcome company. I suppose if the island had been occupied at the time by hippos and crocodiles, we then would have been considered the unwelcome company. Fortunately, all was clear, and upon his return to the boat, he proceeded to set up a folding table. He then draped a tablecloth over it, began setting up an assortment of drinks and food, and placed folding chairs in the sand.

From this breathtaking vantage point in the middle of the Zambezi River, is where we witnessed a stunning sunset while enjoying delicious appetizers and the company of two other wonderful people. It was an unforgettable experience. I only wish the sun had taken longer to set.

Our last day at Chiawa camp was bittersweet. Following a relaxing motor boat cruise on the river, we were met at the dock by a camp staffer and told there had been bad news from home.

Chapter 4: Peace

Immediately, Judy began to panic, thinking something terrible had occurred concerning one of the kids, the house, the dogs, or the business. We were then told about the attack on the Trade Center towers in New York and the subsequent shutdown of all air traffic in the country. Our peace had now been temporarily lost. Judy was out of control, and there was nothing I could do or say to calm her down. Because two of the flights involved in the attack originated in Boston, Judy's anxiety was heightened, and with ten days left in our trip, I had no confidence she would relax. She insisted upon an immediate return home. I tried hard to explain to her we couldn't return home, being that air traffic throughout the country had been ordered suspended. Selfishly, being there was nothing I could affect; I was not willing to sacrifice the remaining ten days of the trip even if it had been possible to return immediately. Fortunately, the camp maintained satellite phone service and we were able to contact the girls, who assured us all was well and secure at home. Only then did she begin to calm down. The last thing I needed was for her to become seriously ill as a result of all the chaos.

The next day, we were scheduled to leave camp for another location. Our bush flight never arrived to transfer us, and that circumstance required being driven to the Zambian capital of Lusaka, where we were brought to a very comfortable hotel for the night. There, we had access to television and were able to watch

BBC news and get visually caught up on happenings pursuant to the tragedy in New York.

Earlier, I think in the previous chapter, I mentioned the oil lamps used to light the pathway to the evening fire, and those hanging from the branches of the nearby trees. The canopy of bright stars in the night sky represented a sea of diamonds. I come back to that simply because it was such a profound influence that I have difficulty putting that evening to sleep in my mind. I promise to move on from that visual. Sometimes I just can't. I remember feeling that, although there was no defense to be had upon the intrusion of lions, leopard, or any other predator who decided to join us by the fire, I was totally at peace under those stars and by the light of those lamps. Rarely had I felt that. There wasn't one second of concern about anything. I remember commenting to my wife that if that intrusion had come to be and the result brought about my demise, I was ok with that end. I know it sounds a bit dramatic, but honestly, I only feel calm and at peace within myself when I'm here. If you've never had the good fortune to experience and enjoy what I've just described to you, I can only say, I'm sorry. Hopefully, if you haven't, at some time and in some special place of your own, you will.

I've come to realize a number of ways peace found its way to me. The night sky, the serenity of the oil lamps, and the African quiet. I'd like to tell you how else I discovered peace and an overwhelming appreciation for where I was and that which appeared before my eyes.

In more recent times, while in Kenya on the Maasai Mara, my guide, Karia, and I left camp quite early one morning. The kitchen had packed things for us to eat in a canvas cool sack, along with coffee and cold drinks. I wanted to stay out in the bush and not return to camp for lunch. As we drove, it wasn't long before we came across a female leopard and her young son.

We guessed the little guy to be nine to twelve months at the time and already quite the athlete. We spent roughly an hour or so watching them interact with each other and then moved on to afford them the privacy of their day. The next morning, we decided to try and locate them, intending to spend a bit more time observing their activities. We were sure to find them being that we knew we were within their established territory. It took a while, but we happened upon them under quite different circumstances.

Somewhat high in a tree were mother and son. The mother had taken an Impala, of course, we didn't know when, but we could see they had already feasted on a portion of it. It appeared to be reasonably fresh, however. Karia positioned the Land Cruiser close to the tree without seeming to have been overly intrusive. Suddenly, mother rose from the tree limb she had been stretched out on, stood at the outermost extent of it, and proceeded to embrace a posture and facial expression that spoke to a grave concern she had. As she stood scanning the open landscape below, it appeared something had alerted her senses to impending danger. She not only had her son to protect but her precious kill as well. As she continued her vigil, the little guy climbed to the half-eaten impala and began having his lunch.

When he was satisfied, he descended the tree and rolled in the fallen leaves while his mother continued her scan of the surroundings. Satisfied there was no apparent threat, she ascended to the kill and skillfully positioned the remains of the impala, made necessary by the little guy having moved it while eating in a manner that compromised its secure position in the tree. It was vital to

Chapter 4: Peace

prevent it from falling from its perch and possibly being lost to scavengers. Here, meals are hard to come by, and solitary hunters such as leopards need to immediately secure any good fortune they have when hunting. Scavengers who traverse the bush in packs are ever-present and don't think twice about confiscating a free and easy meal. It would be considered grand theft in our world. A lone leopard is at great risk trying to defend what's rightfully hers from a team of hungry competitors. She'll need to hunt again, and to do so, cannot be physically compromised in any way, such as due to a confrontation with thieves. Protecting herself from being injured, especially in defense of her kill, becomes paramount. Sometimes it's simply best to walk away when others arrive at the scene too soon.

I tell you this story because the time given to observing this fascinating sequence of events took place over approximately two hours, most of which was having to endure near ninety-degree heat with no shade. No complaints, though. I was so taken by all of this once in a lifetime good fortune, I didn't feel the heat, I erased all else from my mind, and again found a certain inner peace in a totally different forum.

I have to wonder why it takes coming here to find true and honest peace within. It's so strange, it can be found in a place so quiet and yet in a matter of seconds so violent and loud. It's a dynamic that plays over and over in my mind.

Chapter 5: Staying Awake

I commented earlier, I've found it wise to stay awake while in the bush. Wildlife, here as in other places, is opportunistic and doesn't generally give away its intent. Sometimes, not always, it can prove somewhat difficult to read the mood and level of tolerance displayed by a well-taught member of the African wildlife community. I'll attempt to paint a clear picture for you as to how I came to know this to be true. To South Luangwa, Zambia, we go.

Shortly after observing a stunning sunrise one September morning, our guide drove Judy and me deep into a heavily wooded area just off the grassland. As we came around an island of trees, to our left was a male lion with a harem of three ladies. I'd say they were roughly thirty-five yards away and appeared to have recently eaten. I knew because they were all on their backs in the tall grass and not the least bit interested in our being close to them.

Directly ahead, about the same distance from our Land Rover, was a lone lioness lying down facing us with her head resting comfortably on her left front leg, which she had tucked under her chin. She was next to a large bush, half of her on the path we were driving on, her other half in the grass bordering the bush. As we approached her, she suddenly lifted her head and, with concern, cocked it slightly to one side.

I then took notice that her eyes were becoming larger and her stare quite menacing. I heard some sound emanating from the bush the lioness seemed to be guarding, and immediately ordered the guide to stop the car. I told him not to proceed one inch closer to her. His intent had been to drive by her. Seemingly confused, the guide asked the reason for my concern. I told him I wasn't comfortable with the look in her eye, the manner in which she was holding her head, and her general posture. I then asked him if he could hear the sounds emanating from the bush. He listened intently, then turned to me and acknowledged he could. To this day, I'm not sure he recognized the potential danger we were in had he driven closer to the lioness. I told him she belonged to the group we had passed moments ago, and the sounds from the bush were her little ones eating. Just as I said that, the lioness drew her left leg, the one her head had been resting on, into her chest, leading me to believe her intent was to lift herself to a standing position. She was not comfortable with us being there and was not going to tolerate further intrusion. I knew she was preparing to challenge our unwelcome presence. At that moment, protecting her babies was paramount. My fear was, had she risen, so too would the others who were resting in the grass. They undoubtedly would have immediately come to her aid.

The guide simply didn't recognize the potential for a catastrophic event to occur. I then ordered him to slowly reverse the direction of the car and proceed out and around the male and his ladies. He did just that, and as we continued on, I tried, as tactfully as I could, to make him aware how important it was for him to read the moment. Had we driven closer and remained unaware of the concern for her little ones, you might not be reading this. I found it odd that a guide who had been trained and licensed would not have recognized the potential for what could have, and most likely would have been, life-ending. I've come to learn that staying awake and aware at all times is a vital aspect of survival here. It is for the wildlife and should be no less for us who visit.

It would be unfair and quite pompous of me to make you think I was all-knowing and had never taken a snooze while in the African bush. So, full disclosure requires that I relate an incident to you that also occurred while in Zambia.

On an early morning game drive, we happened by what appeared to be something having been dragged along the sandy surface of the ground. Following the trail led us to the base of a tree, and in the tangle of branches above the trunk, there appeared a baboon. Its chest had been opened and feasted upon. It had to have been the work of a hungry leopard who, at this time, was nowhere to be seen. We then positioned ourselves away from the kill and sat for a time, hoping the hunter would return for seconds. We must have sat for thirty or forty minutes. The leopard never returned. We then decided to move on.

As we continued driving, we approached a huge tree on our left. One large limb extended out over the path we were driving on. As we got closer to the limb, our guide suddenly, for what I believed was no discernible reason, accelerated the vehicle, pinning us to the back of our seats. Soon after, just past the limb, he abruptly applied the brakes and stopped. We then were nearly face-planted into the seat divider. Upon asking what the purpose of this maneuver was, the guide casually turned and pointed to the limb. When I turned and looked up,

Chapter 5: Staying Awake

I was shocked to see a leopard napping, quite comfortably, on the low-hanging tree limb. I never saw its tail swishing back and forth as it hung from the tree. By the way, that tree limb was a mere three to four feet above the Land Rover. A very short jump for a hungry leopard. Fortunately for us, the guide was awake. I can't be sure, but most likely this was the cat that took the baboon. I know better than to not look in the trees for leopards. I let my guard down for a moment, and that lapse could have been a monumental mistake. Had the guide been mentally napping and the leopard been hungry, the day may have proven to be a short one. I guess I have the unfortunate baboon to thank. He obviously served to satisfy the leopard's hunger. Staying awake is best to do while here.

One more story, and I promise I'll stop and allow you to catch your breath.

I have a tendency to get excited, having an opportunity to live these life altering experiences over again. They were long in the making and never get old.

A camp I stayed at in Tanzania a few years ago, located in the northern Serengeti, was built into and amongst the huge boulders and rocks of Kogakuria Kopje. It was heavily treed and shared space with dense bushes, some of which enveloped the boulders and large rock formations. I remember there being a lion pride residing just outside camp. Their calls in the dead of night were cause for a difficult attempt at sleep. Dirt pathways, cut through the bush, led to the tents. I can assure you the place was somewhat frightening when the sun went down.

Following dinner one evening, I requested an escort to accompany me to my tent. After sundown, as with most camps, it was mandatory. It was about nine o'clock and I was very tired from the day's activity and needed a good night's sleep. The escort gathered a spear and a lantern, and off we went. We proceeded along the path that led from the dining area to another that led to my tent. As we turned left and proceeded a few steps down the path to the tent, without warning, two cape buffalo appeared from behind a bush and stood side by side facing us. I'd venture to say they were

Chapter 5: Staying Awake

no further than forty or fifty feet from us. Hardly enough distance from which to think about escape from a charge. We immediately stopped, and the standoff commenced. We stared each other down for what seemed like a month, but in real time, it was for a little over five minutes.

I felt somewhat fearful, but at the same time didn't see anything threatening in their behavior. What ultimately made me nervous was watching the escort lowering his spear, dropping the lantern he was carrying, and shifting all his weight to his front leg. He saw something I didn't. I then realized there was only one spear and two buffalo. Something about that was not going to work if a defense became necessary. All of a sudden, for no apparent reason, the two buffalo retreated to behind the bush from where they had emerged.

Knowing we couldn't continue walking to the tent as long as the buffaloes were behind the bush we needed to walk by, the escort picked up a large rock and threw it into the bush to flush the buffaloes out. It worked. They immediately came out from behind the bush, but this time turned away from us and proceeded to make their way down the slope to the side of my tent and on to a grassy area below where they camped for the night.

I'm a believer that having kept our eyes open avoided what could have been a nasty confrontation that may not have ended well. Once again, proof this place is not a zoo. It's for real. It's very real.

For whatever time we spend here, one shouldn't forget whose house we're in.

On a recent trip to Kenya, I stayed at a camp that was established high on a forested hill overlooking a bend in the Mara River. From my tent, a stone walkway led to the open-air main lodge and dining area. It was an uphill walk, but pleasant through the trees. Very early one morning, just prior to the sun breaking the horizon, I left my tent and began making my way along the stone path to the lodge. It wasn't light yet, so I kept my head on a swivel to be aware of what might be wandering through camp. In short order, I heard the faint snap of a tree branch from further up the hill above the path. When I looked in the direction of what I heard, I saw, standing, near upright and watching me, a large lone male baboon. He was staring intently, and I have to say in quite an intimidating manner. I stopped walking and we just stared at each other. At one point, he momentarily displayed his massive teeth. That was all I had to see. I thought it best to continue walking. We both began to walk, he in one direction and me in the opposite direction toward the lodge, never taking our eyes off each other. I represented no competition to him and was thankful to have reached the relative safety of the lodge unscathed. Looking back on that situation, it was not smart to have stopped walking and stare at a lone male baboon who could have charged and folded me like a wallet. I know better than to do that.

Chapter 5: Staying Awake

The fact that he was alone was curious to me. I should have waited until light dawned to leave my tent. Lucky, I guess.

Sometimes, even if you're awake, trouble can arise from unexpected places at inopportune times. Still, the best defense is staying awake and being aware at all times.

I've discovered if you mentally nap too often while you're here, many things not related to wildlife can then find a place in your consciousness. It's so easy to cecum to the quiet. Sometimes, though, it's comforting to turn off all else and simply enjoy the symphony of birds or the sweet scent of wild sage. I've even just stood on the bank of the rushing Ruaha River and watched as it powerfully flowed its way by me. It too provided a symphony of its own. One day, for a reason I have no explanation for, I asked my guide to stop the Land Cruiser and proceeded to fixate on an acacia bush. We drove past them every day, but not once had I ever taken the time to stop and appreciate just how unique they are. The more time I spend here, the easier it becomes to treasure more of this place. There's so much available for one to absorb. It's not a sin to put the wildlife away for a time. Other things can actually prove to be quite soothing and, at the same time, stimulating.

I've been fortunate over the past twenty-seven years to have spent a fair amount of time in multiple places in Africa. Staying awake to see all that's available to you can be, and often times is, extremely tiring. There's so much to see. It could be in the trees, sitting on a rock, lying in the grass, lounging in the river, or simply walking along a path. Sometimes those you've come to see will find you interesting. You find yourself not wanting to miss anything. Even though days seem relatively quiet most of the time, there's always something happening that's worth the time to stop and observe. It never ceases to amaze me, the extent to which a place so unlike the environment I live within has captured my heart and soul. All these years later, the thought that to see it once would be enough has proven laughable.

Chapter 6:
On Being Witness

I would venture to say, through the years, I've seen every documentary film ever produced having to do with Africa's wildlife. Most have been fascinating, well put together, and unquestionably exciting. They, in combination with the Nat Geo magazines I discussed in an earlier chapter, were the inspiration for what became my obsession with this truly unique place on earth. In my humble opinion, the BBC ranks number one. They're tireless in their pursuit of the best content. In recent years, I've been privileged to witness their highly skilled people at work. You can feel the extent to which they emotionally connect with the wildlife they've come to record. They're a group who could teach a class in the art of patience.

When you've watched as much wildlife documentary TV as I have, there's a great deal you come to take for granted. I always expected to see elephants roaming in herds across the open plains, frolicking in the rivers, or separating small branches from trees and enjoying a snack. Always exciting was watching a cheetah pursue an impala, take it down in a cloud of dust, cut off its ability to breathe, and drag it to where it could be hidden and protected from scavengers. It all happened so quickly. Then there's usually footage of vultures, always in a chaotic frenzy, competing for the remains of the lion's good fortune, having successfully ended a wildebeest to feast upon.

From the comfort of a recliner, it's relatively easy to enjoy the content of the program without having to allow yourself becoming emotionally involved in what you're watching. After all, you're far enough away that you can't smell any of the carnage, you can't hear all of what's happening, and you're just too distant to experience the nuances of events in their entirety.

I relate it to the difference between watching a sporting event on television and occupying a seat in the stadium while the game is being played. The two venues are worlds apart. One is convenient, the other is real. To further my point, I'll attempt to describe a few instances that I experienced firsthand. None were pleasant, all were very real.

Late October, 2018, I arrived in Tanzania and began a stay in the northern Serengeti. It was my first trip to East Africa, and from the first day, I knew it was going to be an overwhelming fourteen days. I had scheduled this time of year with the hope I'd be fortunate enough to witness the last of the annual Mara River crossings of wildebeest, zebra, and others from Tanzania into Kenya. I had seen this mass migration many times in countless documentaries; now it needed to be for real. I would finally have my seat in the stadium.

Chapter 6: On Being Witness

Upon my arrival at camp, I was told by some that this late in the season could prove to be too late to see crossings. The start of the season is generally in July. I wasn't discouraged, though; I had a good feeling I would witness that which I had come to see. The morning of my first full day in camp, my guide, Joel, took me on a leisurely drive across the savannah to familiarize me with the general landscape. As we drove, there were giraffes gliding along on their way to who knows where. A few lions were rolling in the grass, stretching, performing their morning ritual. Hot air balloons were slowly rising in the sky. Flame from their burners provided a short, periodic glow of light as they rose higher in the sky. Baboons were moving about, some with little ones on their backs, walking with a great deal of purpose. It reminded me of mothers walking their kids to catch the morning school bus. Quite a bit of activity, to say the least. As the sun rose in the sky, I could sense the day was about to become serious.

Mid-morning, we parked under a tree, put out a couple of folding chairs, had coffee, and enjoyed some morning deliciousness. I can't begin to tell you how relaxing it was. Again, so quiet and peaceful. Suddenly, the radio in the Land Cruiser began to crackle with word of a potential crossing at a particular location along the river. We quickly folded the chairs, put the snacks away, and off we went. We drove maybe fifteen minutes during which time we could see the wildebeest and zebra frantically making their way to the river. The dust rising from their pounding hoofs was blocking the sun. They were coming from everywhere, nonstop.

Being that all this activity was originating from the Tanzanian side of the river, we needed to cross to the Kenyan side. From that vantage point, they would be crossing toward us. There was a low, narrow concrete bridge not far from where the herds were gathering. We made our way across, took a position, and waited for the activity to begin. The number of animals making their way to the river was countless and seemed never-ending. Crocodiles were now exposing themselves, arriving in numbers of their own and patiently waiting for an opportunity to hunt.

For no apparent reason, the wildebeest turned and made their way to another crossing point. I remember it being a reasonable distance from where we were, but why did they move? This happened four or five times over an hour and a half or so. Each time they would move further away then begin the back and forth along the bank of the river. We followed each time they moved. In the end, they returned to where we were originally positioned. Joel couldn't explain it. He told me it's just what they do. Finally, one jumped into the river, and the game was on. Hundreds of wildebeest, zebra, and other antelope entered the river and began the treacherous journey across the mighty Mara in search of fresh grass, just as happens for a few months every year.

Chapter 6: On Being Witness

Once in the water, it becomes a roll of the dice as to who will be chosen by a croc. Life came to an abrupt end for many that day. I sat watching this monumental event taking place before my eyes and was taken by the water being shaken off onto me by the wildebeest as those fortunate to have survived the army of crocodiles exited the river and made their way past our vehicle. Then, I saw it happen. I caught the eyes of a croc just above the surface of the water. It was on a mission and appeared to have chosen its' prey. The crocodile was now within striking distance and, in an instant, burst from below the surface of the river with its jaws wide open and proceeded to close on and secure the midsection of an unsuspecting wildebeest it had focused upon. Next on the crocodile's agenda was to drown the animal. From my vantage point, I could hear the agonizing cries from the wildebeest.

I could see the pain on its face as the croc began to force it below the surface of the water. It was totally out of its element, and there was no way in hell it could defend itself. Slowly, it began to disappear into the depths of the river. I heard one last cry, witnessed one last breath, and it disappeared. It all happened so quickly and within the midst of the most chaotic environment I've ever witnessed. So many animals, so tightly packed together, churning an enormous volume of water and disregarding peril in pursuit of fresh, life sustaining grass. No monetary value could ever be established for the acquisition of a seat in this stadium.

Chapter 6: On Being Witness

The event was life-altering for me. I may be repeating myself, but as many times as I've watched the taking of a zebra or wildebeest from the comfort of my recliner, having seen it happen with my eyes, hearing it with my ears, and smelling it through my nose, all from less than a football field away, I must tell you it seemed well beyond life-altering. I captured still images that to this day are difficult to look at without stirring emotions I don't need to recall. They certainly don't provoke a smile.

For the balance of that day, I played that depressing event over and over in my mind. I felt what I witnessed couldn't have been real. It was impossible to appreciate anything I saw the remainder of the day. I couldn't sleep and at times felt seeing that heart-wrenching event through my mind's eye was beginning to eat my brain. To this very day, I see the agony on the face of that wildebeest, I hear the cry of pain, and the visual of its disappearance under the water is the most haunting of all. It happened so quickly. Perspective gained from a seat in this stadium can change you. Trust me. I don't want anyone to begin thinking I'm naive. I'm well aware and understand nature possesses its own playbook, and things don't happen for no reason. I knew why this horror needed to occur, though that understanding didn't seem to influence the effect it had upon me this particular day. I don't think I'll be buying season tickets to this event anytime soon.

The following week I camped in southern Tanzania in a region known as Selous. The camp had been established on the Ruaha River. Not many people visited this region. I was told because it was somewhat inconvenient to get to and was not too well promoted. Just the kind of place I enjoy most. I pretty much had camp to myself for the week I was there. My first order of business upon arrival was to establish a friendly relationship with the chef. I did just that, and upon my return home, blew up my bathroom scale. Joseph, the guide who had been assigned to me, was amazing. He was extremely knowledgeable, accommodating, and communicative. We enjoyed our days together. The landscape was heavily forested and was certainly not void of wildlife. There was nothing I didn't like about this camp or the environment.

Joseph and I, at my request, spent a great deal of time at the river. It was teeming with activity for a good part of the day. Countless hippos, crocodiles galore, and more lions than I expected to see. Before I get to the serious stuff, I'd like to share with you an unexpected, amusing encounter Joseph and I came to enjoy the entire week I was there.

We were required to return to camp every day before dark. We were not armed, and there was enough violent activity that occurred when the sun went down to make that necessary. Wildlife in this remote region were not accustomed to seeing people regularly and

Chapter 6: On Being Witness

therefore were less tolerant of human presence. That said, late one afternoon, while returning to camp, we stopped to explore a den that had been dug at the base of an enormous Baobab tree. The den appeared to have been abandoned, but as we sat and talked, at a distance we saw two warthogs in a leisurely trot coming our way through the forest. We decided to sit and watch to discern specifically where they were headed.

At what appeared to be a pre-determined place, both made a left turn, and shortly after, made another left turn and proceeded to head toward where we were parked. It was near dark at this point, but neither of us was thinking about getting back to camp. We were fixated on these two hogs, and our seats were too good to give up. It was as if they were returning home from work. All of a sudden, one of the pair emerged from behind a bush not far from us, scampered across the path in front of us, and took a position in front of the den. Obviously, this was home. She then turned, backed down into the empty den, came back out, and with her snout began tossing loose dirt at us. She seemed quite annoyed that we had invited ourselves to her home.

In all my time in Africa, I never experienced that level of disrespect. We weren't more than five yards from the entry to that den. It was a very personal encounter and one that put an enormous smile on our faces. Quite comedic to say the least. Anyway, when it was determined the coast was clear and we weren't a threat, her husband joined her, and we went on our way. The balance of my stay, we stopped there every night on our way back to camp. Their nightly routine never differed. Not one bit. I think they had even accepted us. It made me wish my stay could have been longer.

One absolutely beautiful November night, I was sitting on the dining deck overlooking the river under a magnificent blanket of stars. Some were occasionally dancing across the sky. Shooting stars, I'd never seen them before. I was preparing to have dinner

Chapter 6: On Being Witness

when the camp manager made his way up the stairs that led to the deck, holding a lantern and in somewhat of a frenzy, told me to follow him. I told him I had just begun to have dinner, to which he replied, "Come now, I'll have the kitchen prepare another dinner for you". We proceeded down the steps, around the bamboo fence surrounding the kitchen, and stopped to watch two female lions who were in a deliberate slow trot approaching camp. They were not a safe distance away. They did, however, seem laser-focused on what I knew was a trip to the river. Even when the light was turned on them, they never looked or broke their gate. They disappeared into the night, and I returned to the deck and enjoyed dinner. The manager sat with me for a short time and we talked about a few things. He was a very nice guy and I enjoyed his company. I did take the liberty to respectfully tell him I didn't think it had been wise for us to have been in close proximity to two lions who were obviously out hunting. He never responded to my concern. To be perfectly honest, the experience was exhilarating. There's something very special about African nights.

After dinner, I asked to be escorted to my tent. Once secure within, I was preparing for bed, at which time I began hearing a strange sound emanating from the area of the river. It was a cry, the sound of distress, and I must admit, quite daunting to listen to. Something was experiencing great pain. I listened intently as the cries continued for approximately fifteen minutes. As fast as they began, they ceased. I tried to sleep but found it impossible to do so; I couldn't seem to quell the sounds of those fifteen minutes from my mind.

While attempting to force myself to sleep, I began to think about what took place at the river during the day. The hippos were in the river most of the time, avoiding the sun, the crocodiles were lounging on the sandbars in the river, taking an occasional swim, and then there was the recollection of a lone lioness who rested in the grass just off the sand on an elevated plateau. During late afternoon, as the sun would get lower in the sky, the hippos would exit the river and leisurely walk to where they could begin feeding on the vegetation and later bed down for the night. All was calm and quite peaceful. Then it came to me. The lone lioness was there to choose which of the hippos they might take when darkness prevailed. I got out of bed and began walking around inside the tent, and as I did, more and more of the puzzle came together. The two lionesses trotting through camp earlier were on their way to the river to take the hippo chosen that afternoon by the scout who had been resting on the plateau. I'm sure they jumped the unsuspecting giant and immediately began the process of disabling it, most likely by attempting to sever its spinal cord. I had no way to be sure that's what prompted the earlier cries, but that analysis allowed me the luxury of being able to return to bed and fall asleep.

Chapter 6: On Being Witness

The following morning, Joseph and I set out on our drive and had a very productive day. The wildlife sightings were many, and the photo opportunities endless. As night was falling upon us, we started back to camp, and on the way, I told Joseph to drive to the river. Again, he reminded me it was getting dark and we were required to be in camp. I assured him I would take responsibility for any reprimand. This day, the warthogs we came to be friends with would have a reprieve. Time was not going to permit our nightly visit.

Reluctantly, he drove to the river, whereupon I instructed him to proceed along the shoreline, which he did. Sure enough, there was the hippo on its' back, belly up. I'm sure during the night when jumped by the lions it instinctively made its' way back to the river to escape the attack, but had been compromised to the extent survival was impossible. The lions' hunt had failed. Joseph and I counted twenty-seven crocodiles feeding on the remains. The tearing of flesh from the dead hippo was extremely difficult to watch. The odor was equally pervasive. In two days, that hippo was gone. All that remained was the remnant of a once magnificent giant.

I believe my interest and obsession with this incident effected Joseph in a way he had never thought about. I made him aware of the process that led to the hippo's demise, beginning with the lone lion resting on the plateau earlier in the day. I could tell I had triggered an awareness. He was very quiet and thoughtful, totally out of character. He listened intently to my chronology of events regarding this recent lion hippo relationship. Until now, he may not have ever thought about or experienced any emotion when observing an event similar to what we saw that day. I'm not sure he ever considered the entire process from beginning to end. I hope I taught him how to establish the pieces of a puzzle.

My first journey to Kenya took place in 2021. It was a scheduled ten-day stay at two camps and was focused on time spent within the Maasai Mara National Park. At one camp, I had the good fortune to be guided by a well-known, accomplished Maasai gentleman, Jackson Looseyia. Jackson knew every square inch of this park, and I can assure you nothing escaped the telescopic quality of his eyes. He saw things that all this time later I'd still be looking for. He went nowhere without his binoculars. I was never convinced he needed them. They seemed almost a prop.

One beautiful sunny day, Jackson suggested that we drive to an area referred to as the marsh to see if we could locate a well-established resident pride of lions. We drove to the marsh, and as luck would have it, they were home. They had recently taken an elderly male cape buffalo and were feeding on it when we arrived. The buffalo was massive and might have been taken during the night, given that most of it was intact. Jackson positioned the Land

Chapter 6: On Being Witness

Cruiser just a few yards from the head of the buffalo. The flies were unbearable, and the smell from the partially eaten carcass was enough to make you want to pass out. It must have taken a number of lions to take this huge animal down. I'm sure they began feasting while still in the process of doing so. The remaining expression on its face told a story of excruciating pain and suffering. A violent, but necessary end.

All these violent goings on tear at your heart and mind, and it's not easy to remind yourself of the need for it to take place. There is a reason and purpose for it all. I don't think any of it that I've seen over the past twenty-seven years could ever be forgotten. I've observed, on the faces of those who are native to this special place, a certain degree of pain when we happen upon a scene similar to what I just described, but they understand the reason and the need for what they see. Here, it's simply to do with respect. Respect for the land, the wildlife, each other, and the gift of life itself. People here perceive and accept these virtues. For me, in its totality, there can be no greater place on earth.

Chapter 7:
Images

I'm quite sure, in an earlier chapter, I referenced never having owned a camera or taken photographs prior to my first trip to Africa. Photography was an activity that was of no interest to me. Upon making plans to visit, I realized traveling halfway around the world to fulfill a lifelong dream was going to require returning with images of what I saw while there. Off to the photo shop I went. Thirty-five millimeter was the standard at the time. Digital photography was in its' infancy. In the event one might fail or somehow malfunction, I bought two camera bodies, one seventy-five to three hundred mm lens, and a good quality camera bag to protect the investment. I relied totally on the photo shop salesperson's expertise, not having a clue what to do otherwise. He then graciously gave me some basic instructions on the use of the equipment. In the end, all his advice proved spot on. When it came to film, I again sought his counsel, and he recommended three different film speeds and schooled me under what circumstances to use each. Available light was the primary determining factor.

Upon arrival at our first camp, I loaded both camera bodies, each with a different speed film. Changing the lens from one to the other was easy enough to do and only took seconds to accomplish. Off we went on a late afternoon game drive.

Something very interesting happened on that drive. Earlier, I mentioned having brought forty-two rolls of film and returned home, only having shot twenty-three of the forty-two. Never having been a patient individual, I found myself being very selective about the photos I took. Selective in the sense that I discovered the patience to wait for the shot and took the time necessary to frame and compose it to my liking. To this day, I have no idea from where that patience came. Once home, I took the twenty-three rolls of film I shot to have them developed. The photo processor called me when he completed the processing and told me to come immediately to look at the four by six prints. He seemed very excited and told me he'd never seen photos as well taken as mine. They did seem to be well done, and I was very appreciative of the processor's kind words.

This first trip turned out to be one of personal discovery. In addition to having framed my shots well, I found I had been very steady. Only a half dozen prints displayed blur. I never gave holding the camera steady a thought. There have been numerous discoveries made about myself on these many journeys to Africa. It's a unique place that evokes discovery to surface from the depths in which it resides within you.

Early one morning, while at our first camp and following a light breakfast, we set out on a game drive with our guide, Busi. We drove a while and saw the morning activities of many smaller species, who seemed so busy it led all of us to think maybe there's not going to be enough time in the day for them to complete their tasks. How much could they have to do? Anyway, we continued driving, and as luck would have it, we came upon a family of cheetahs.

Mother and her four little ones were sleeping under a large tree and at the base of a termite mound that was surrounded by huge bushes. It was a place that appeared to offer them a degree of safety and security from intruders. We decided to sit by them for a while, hoping they would wake up and get busy.

Chapter 7: Images

After sitting about forty-five minutes in the same place, Busi suggested we move on. I politely asked him to stay where we were a while longer. The setting was too good to chance missing anything. Five minutes later, I sensed the mother was about to awaken and begin the day. I put the camera to my eye and sure enough she sat up and positioned herself in a Hollywood like pose, allowing me an opportunity to capture an image that was made of the stuff I could only have dreamed of. That said, now I was going to have to wait two weeks to see just how good it was. That's the issue with film. In the end, that photograph proved perfectly composed and could not have been any more sharp. The colors are stunning.

We waited a bit longer only to see the mother teaching her little ones the art of stalking prey. A warthog had walked from a treed area to the open grassland. The warthog was too far away for her to run down and may have been too big for her to take. I think the exercise was more to do with teaching her young the first chapter of the hunt.

As the sun began to climb in the sky, the opportunities to capture color-rich images were disappearing. There were still circumstances that allowed for good-quality shots, but not many. It was ok, though. Not much happened midday. It was too hot for most to remain active. Late afternoon, as did early morning, offered perfect light and opportunities to shoot great photographs.

Game viewing drives at night can either be very boring or so exciting it becomes difficult to catch your breath. I don't do them anymore. At my age, by day's end, I'm generally too exhausted from the day's activities and prefer a nice quiet dinner and a relaxing glass of Amarula by a raging fire before retiring to bed. When I was younger, I looked forward to those drives at night. Many camps don't offer game drives after dark anymore. A number of the national parks in East Africa will not permit vehicles to travel within the parks through the evening hours for reasons of safety and to afford the wildlife privacy and the unobtrusive freedom to conduct their nightly business.

While in Botswana, we set out one evening on a drive, hoping to see a leopard hunting. Our tracker, securely positioned on the left front fender of the vehicle, was shining his spotlight into the bush from one side of the Land Rover to the other as we drove along slowly so as not to miss anything that might be of interest. At a fair distance ahead, the tracker suddenly sat up perfectly straight, positioned his light into the tall grass that was swaying somewhat violently back and forth, pointed, and told the guide to drive into where the grass was waving. There was virtually no breeze that night to influence movement of the grass, so something had to be happening.

Chapter 7: Images

As we drove into and through the grass, there appeared a small clearing occupied by four frenzied hyenas who had just taken down an adult warthog. They were in the process of violently tearing the hog to pieces. I remember being so mesmerized by what was happening before my eyes. Even with all the light available from the trackers' spotlight and headlamps from the Land Rover, I never gave a thought to picking up my camera and photographing the carnage. At one point, one of the hyenas dove into the chest cavity of the hog, tore a large section of flesh and bone away, and disappeared into the tall grass to feast upon it. I recall so vividly the sound of it being torn from its' body. It was as if someone was tearing apart a pair of blue jeans. Twenty-seven years later, and I can hear it as if it were happening right this minute. Within thirty minutes, that warthog was gone. Bone and all. For the next hour or so, I was rendered speechless.

Judy and the girls had no interest in dinner after witnessing that event. I couldn't blame them. While in bed, not being able to sleep right away, as tired as I was, I asked myself why I hadn't photographed any of that thirty minutes. Available light was not an issue. I was never able to answer that question. What I had realized was the delicate balance that exists between the importance of sometimes observing the moment as opposed to attempting to capture an image on film. That night, I chose to secure the image in my head. Maybe because I knew it would never be lost or destroyed. It would remain secure within the vault of my mind.

Photo opportunities are endless in Africa. This place is a candy store of chances to return home with unique images available nowhere else on earth. I've done that. Several of the guides I've had over the years have commented negatively on my wanting to sit so long in one place and on one subject. The argument by most had roots in the belief that too much time spent in one place was allowing escape of many other possibilities to capture great things. I admit there's truth to that, and it's a valid point. What they don't take into consideration is the desire and need for me to observe and better understand the subjects I choose to photograph. I have no interest in a hit-and-run approach to my time in the bush. I want to depart this magnificent place each time with as many mind images of the wildlife and their behavior as I do images in print. Too many come to Africa and leave not having taken the time to live Africa. I don't care to be one of them. It's too important to me.

At one camp in Kenya, I met a nice couple from the States. In conversation, the wife asked how many times I'd visited Africa. I told her, and she then asked if, after being there a number of times through the years, had I acquired an affection for one specific animal. I told her that leopards, females in particular, were of great interest to me. Her next question was an expected why that was.

Chapter 7: Images

I replied by telling her I was impressed with the complexity of the solitary life a female leopard must deal with. I brought to her attention the leopard's unending responsibility to mate, give birth, feed, teach, and defend her young while alone with no one to help or defend her. The process taking place over fifteen to maybe twenty months, possibly losing one or two along the way. Then, she must mate and do it all over again. Impressive to say the least. She shares a similar life to her friend, the cheetah.

I speak to this because every day for a week, I had the privilege to not only photograph but observe a beautiful, strong, healthy female leopard and her lone son. The young one we guessed was ten to fourteen months at the time, and it wouldn't be that much longer before mother and young would part ways and most likely never see each other again. I watched them play with each other. Each time they did, I could see the mother imparting her skills upon her offspring. Teaching moments amidst the frolicking. At one point, I observed the mother in a low crouch moving through the grass, her playful little one halting its activity and watching with great interest. I can't say for sure, but my best guess would be this was a lesson in the proper posture from which to stalk. Another day, I saw the mother taking the young one to the ground repeatedly with a swipe from her left and sometimes right paw. Maybe a teaching moment in the art of the takedown of prey. There's more to see here than a camera can capture. There are times one simply has to take time to use the lens of the eye, deposit and lock that image in the mind, as I occasionally do.

There have been many photo opportunities that came about totally unexpectedly, but fortunately at a good time. Early one morning, my guide Karia and I were leisurely driving within the Naboisho Conservancy in Kenya when we decided to stop for no particular reason. Strangely, not too much was happening that morning, at least in the area we were scouting. Directly ahead of our vehicle, about eight to ten yards, was an acacia bush. My camera was sitting on my lap. Karia and I were engaged in some conversation when, from seemingly nowhere, a Lilac-Breasted Roller landed on the acacia bush in front of the Land Cruiser. If you've never seen one of these birds, I can only describe them as quite colorful and luminous. Their feathers are a mix of brown, aqua, tan, lilac, and a hint of blue. Vibrant might be the best way to describe the colors. They generally don't sit very long when they land, so I had to get the camera to my eye, focus, compose the shot, and pray this magnificent bird would sit still long enough for me to capture it. I think it must have known that because it remained perched on the bush just long enough for me to get one shot. In the time it took to take the camera away from my eye, it was gone. The photo image, titled "Luminous," is amazing and can be seen on the Portrait Gallery page of my website.

(theandoniangallery.com)

You might wonder, how many photos of lions do you need to take? Or how many leopards, cheetahs, etc., etc.. It's a fair question. I can only tell you that in twenty-seven years of photographing wildlife in Africa, no one image of the same species is common to another. What an amazing place this is. Different every time. So much influences every photo you take here.

While on the plane on my way to Tanzania in 2018, I remember thinking how unbelievable it would be to come upon three or four young lion cubs sitting side by side looking out at the savannah. It would be of no consequence where they were sitting. It could be on a fallen tree, on a boulder, in the grass, or maybe innocently sitting by their mother. It wouldn't matter. I caught myself smiling and hoped no one had been looking at me. The reality was, that photo opportunity was never going to present itself. I've never been that lucky in my entire life. My smile disappeared quickly, and I then began thinking about things unrelated to the trip.

I arrived in Tanzania late in the evening and was transferred to a wonderful lodge for an overnight stay before being flown to camp the next morning. Upon arrival at camp, I was shown my tent, unpacked my things, and made my way to the main lodge to meet my guide. I had a quick lunch and left camp for the balance of the day. We saw a number of interesting things, and at one point the guide said we should try to locate a pride of resident lions who had four two-month-old cubs. I said, "lets do it", and off we went. It took some time, but we found them sleeping atop a massive boulder that was canopied by trees and bushes that over the years had grown up and around it. It offered a perfect vantage point from where the lionesses could scout the savannah for prey and provided protective cover for the little ones. We sat for quite a while waiting for the cubs to awaken and hopefully find their way to the ground to begin playing. It never happened. They did awaken but remained atop the boulder. The canopy of green was so thick we could only see glimpses of them as they chased each other around the top of the enormous rock. We stayed for an hour and a half, maybe two hours, and decided we'd try again the following day. We continued on our way, and I have to say the balance of the day was very productive. I

Chapter 7: Images

was able to collect a number of great shots encompassing an array of wildlife and stunning landscapes.

The next morning, I was totally focused on spending time with this lion pride. As we left camp, there was a sunrise beginning to occur, unlike any I had ever seen. We were just outside camp, and I asked the guide to stop so I could photograph the sun beginning to rise from just below the horizon. It was magnificent, a fire in the sky, and a great start to the day. As we moved on, the light was encouraging me to take advantage of some opportunities, and I certainly did. There appeared a handsome male lion sitting comfortably by himself, scanning the surroundings from behind a large rock.

He appeared to have been recently coiffed and permitted us such close access, I believe, had I extended my hand, we could have greeted each other with a cordial handshake. The suns' position in the sky draped him in gold. His pose was begging me to capture a portrait shot. No way was I going to let this opportunity escape. I took the shot, thanked him, and we moved on. My heart was beating so hard and so fast, I wasn't sure I'd make it through the rest of the day. This may have been the most personal wildlife encounter I can remember. I know it's one I'll never forget.

When we arrived at the infamous huge bolder, we discovered the young lions on the ground playing and being an enormous pain in their mother's neck. They were crawling all over her, biting her tail, jumping on her back. I'm sure some of what they were doing was instinctual. Things they would need to do when they matured and joined the hunt. She was so tolerant. I guess that's just what mothers have to be. Anyway, we again spent quite a bit of time with them and at one point decided to leave them and return later in the day.

When we did return, mid-afternoon, the fantasy image I had in my mind while on the plane to Tanzania had come to be. There they were, all four sitting side by side on the boulder that was their home, looking out over the savannah below.

Chapter 7: Images

It was exactly the scene I saw in my mind while on the plane. They must have gone for a swim at some point during the day; all four were still wet. I was stunned, and it took a minute to realize it was happening for real. I got the camera to my eye, took the shots I wanted, proceeded to take a deep breath, and could have cared less what might happen the rest of the day.

By day's end, I was emotionally drained and confused as to why such good fortune was bestowed upon me this one day. I can't remember that ever happening to me. Thank God for Amarula. I was certainly going to need a taste by the fire this night.

Light, expression, pose, location. I could go on and on. Take my word for it, no two African photo opportunities are ever alike. It's one of many enticements that draw me here time and again. Seductive, that best describes what this place is.

I don't want to forget the landscapes. They, too, are as breathtaking as the wildlife that inhabits them.

Chapter 7: Images

They are equally as diverse as all other components of this environment. There are wide, winding rivers everywhere. An inland delta and desert in Botswana. Desert, mountains, and a long Atlantic Ocean shoreline in Namibia. Never-ending savannah throughout Kenya and Tanzania. Thick forests and bushland. Beautiful coastline where the Atlantic and Indian oceans join hands in South Africa, and equally gorgeous Indian Ocean coast along eastern Kenya and Tanzania. There are no words to describe the abundance of everything here.

I only hope the coming years will be kind and allow me the good fortune to explore the Africa I have yet to see.

Chapter 8: Native People

While in Africa, I've allocated a great deal of my schedule to observing and trying to come to know the people who see to it that my time here is nothing short of overwhelming. They have treated me with the utmost respect, shared their knowledge of the bush, and unknowingly taught me the oftentimes lost virtue of a smile. I think earlier, I briefly spoke to how confusing it can be trying to understand the seeming non-stop conversation that takes place among the native people. When I reference non-stop it's just that, non-stop. Their lives simply don't appear to be comprised of the complexity that would inspire such a need to converse. I guess in the end, it's all relative.

In East Africa, most of the camps are staffed by Maasai people. Swahili is their native language, and I will tell you I could listen to it all day, every day, the rest of my life. There's something about the cadence that agrees with me. It's fast and exciting. I regret not speaking it. I think if I were here more often and for longer periods of time, I'd make it a priority to learn what I perceive to be a powerful and magical language. I commend the many Maasai I've spent time with here for their having put forth the effort to learn my native tongue. They speak it well. Communication here has never been an issue.

It's always been interesting to me that within the bush, a place generally void of vibrant color, there exists among the people a kaleidoscope of color. The ladies inject an abundance of bright color into the handmade beaded bracelets and neckwear they produce. The patterns of beads are quite artistic. Long dresses worn by women are equally patterned, bright, and colorful as are shukas and wraps used to keep people warm in the evening. It speaks to their appreciation of life and a great spiritual awareness.

While at a camp in Kenya that was in a wildlife-rich area, I was escorted to and from my tent day and night by a Maasai fellow who spoke no English. There was such a profusion of wildlife roaming in the area and freely throughout camp at all times that it was considered unsafe for anyone to walk about unaccompanied. Lucas, armed with only his spear, which I never saw him without, was extremely protective of me, and to spite the fact he spoke no English and I no Swahili, we communicated quite well. It was a lot of hand gesturing, head nodding, pointing, and smiling. My tent was quite a long way from the main lodge, so I understood the concern for not wanting me to be wandering about by myself.

Chapter 8: Native People

Lucas seemed to embrace the responsibility of ensuring my safety. He shadowed my every move when I was anywhere in camp. One day, following a morning game drive, I had a light lunch and wanted to get to my tent to catch a nap before heading out on an afternoon drive. Lucas escorted me through camp to my tent, at which time I pointed to my watch to let him know when to return and accompany me back to the lodge. He nodded, we shook hands as we always did, and I entered the tent and stretched out on the bed. I assumed Lucas would return to the lodge. I was wrong. He spent the next two hours standing by my tent, waiting for me to awaken so he could guide me safely to the dining area. How's that for being dedicated? I wish I could have brought him home.

The day before I was scheduled to leave camp, my guide Karia, Lucas, and I were standing together on the lawn at the lodge. I captured a few pictures of Karia and Lucas before asking a staff member to get a shot of the three of us together. I then proceeded to assemble the kitchen staff and other camp personnel to have them pose for a few remembrances. They were all quite willing to do so. My stay culminated with a fantastic dinner that evening by the calming light of oil lamps. The next morning, I was preparing to leave camp.

Karia was tasked with driving me some two and a half hours through the bush to my next camp. It was a fantastic drive. I saw, first hand, Maasai tending their livestock, their villages, and most impressive, young Maasai children playing and quite happy to be

Chapter 8: Native People

doing so. Prior to leaving Lucas, Karia, and the camp manager, Richard and I were standing by the Land Cruiser talking when Lucas said something to Karia in Swahili, which immediately brought about a chuckle from both. I asked what was so funny, and Karia proceeded to tell me Lucas was enamored with my not having any hair. He then asked Karia if he could feel the top of my head. Karia, laughing, not quite vociferously, asked me if it would be ok if Lucas felt the top of my head. Could I have said no to him? Of course not. I lowered my head, he felt the hairless crown, and began laughing like a five-year-old. It wouldn't surprise me to learn he's still laughing and rolling in the grass. I'll bet he found my protruding front equally amusing. I don't think he dared go near that one, though. Anyway, it was fun knowing my lack of hair provided the impetus for Lucas to enjoy a good laugh before I left. Such wonderful people. The photographs I have of them are cherished possessions, and it never seems to get old looking at them from time to time.

Earlier, I referenced having a guide while in Kenya by the name of Jackson. For the week he and I were together exploring the Maasai Mara, we engaged in a great deal of conversation. Jackson is extremely intelligent and energetic. Our discussions were nothing short of enlightening and informative. It would be impossible to ever think you could have enough time with this wonderful man.

While on a drive late one morning, we were forced to stop by a low concrete bridge that spanned a shallow crossing point at a river. Two Maasai men were tending to a herd of cattle and approached the river crossing about the same time we did. Jackson pulled off the path we were driving on and stopped to allow the herd to cross the bridge. While waiting, we sat and talked, and at one point, my eyes caught sight of a woman standing in the river washing clothes. It was so interesting to me to see her doing laundry in the river and tossing it onto the rocks along the bank to dry in the sun. All this activity in one isolated place at the same time. It seemed so primitive. I began to wonder how far that woman had to walk through the bush with her laundry to wash it in the river. She then would have to make that same journey home. How long had those Maasai men driven that cattle herd to the point of the river crossing, and how much further was their journey going to be? What about their return? I would remind you, all on foot. I remember commenting to Jackson just how pure Africa this was to me. So often it's the unexpected encounter that proves to be most impactful. It certainly was to me this day.

As we proceeded on our drive, Jackson made mention of having observed how intently I had watched the goings on at the river and how quiet I had become. I told him it was the simplicity of the moment and what it represented that impressed me. It spoke directly to where I was. This was an African people moment.

Chapter 8: Native People

Jackson began telling me about a woman who had recently been washing clothes in another section of the same river. She had brought her young boy and a friend along so they could play in the water while she did the wash. While the boys played, unexpectedly, a crocodile appeared and in an instant ended the young son's life. He simply disappeared below the surface of the water. I had to wonder how many times the mother had done a wash in that same place in the river, and how often the kids played there with no consequence. I think Jackson was comfortable telling me of that incident because he knew to what degree I understood the realities of life in the bush. I think he saw the seriousness of my wanting and needing to be there.

One day, under a somewhat ominous sky, Jackson and I were sitting in the Land Cruiser by a tree in which a male leopard was napping. It's fun to watch them in the act of trying to change their position on the limb they're sleeping on. It can appear to be clumsy, I can assure you it's anything but. We sat for some time, hoping he'd wake up and do something, anything. He was a big boy, and when he did awaken, he gave no indication he was happy to see us. He did finally descend the tree and upon contacting the ground, yawned, displaying dagger like k9's. As he walked by the vehicle, he stared with an uninviting stare, and if looks could kill, we were dead. I don't ever remember seeing a leopard that large. I'd venture a guess and say he was a very astute hunter, one who enjoyed great success doing so.

Chapter 8: Native People

While we were waiting for the leopard to awaken, Jackson told me about a relative of his, an uncle, I believe, who left the village one day to camp in the bush for a time. He never told anyone where he intended to establish camp. He never returned. People from the village searched for him, but not knowing the general vicinity of his travels, were unsuccessful in their quest to find him. It seemed a mystery. He was Maasai and, having been raised in the bush, was knowledgeable about his environment. The Mara is a seemingly never-ending expanse of territory, but how far could he have travelled on foot? Sometime later, I can't remember just how long, someone came to the village and told of clothing that was discovered tangled within the branches of a tree in a particular location. Upon inspection by relatives of the missing man, it was determined the clothes belonged to him. It appeared to be the deed of a hungry leopard. At that point, the mystery had been solved.

Terrible things can happen here, even to those who are native and well-versed in the order of things. I know the more time I spend here and listen to the stories told to me by native people, the more I understand and respect the relationship between wildlife and humans. In the end, it's amazing how well it all seems to work, most of the time.

Zambia, 2001. Following a somewhat contentious experience at a small airstrip with a less than cordial passport control person,

Judy and I were going to be driven to a camp for a three-night stay. I can't remember how long the drive was going to be, I was just glad to be done with that moronic passport control guy. He was upset because our flight into Zambia had been late arriving. I guess he had more important things to do and was annoyed having to wait for us. I must say, I kept myself under control and gave him no opportunity to exercise his desire to make life miserable for Judy and me.

A very nice young English lady was waiting for us, and as soon as we cleared passport control, she welcomed us to Zambia, and our drive to camp was underway. I wish I could recall her name, but my memory won't permit that. She was extremely pleasant, I do remember that. The drive was uneventful except for a great deal of uplifting and informative conversation with the driver. At one point, we came upon greenery that had been placed along the center of the road, at which time our driver slowed to a crawl and purposely avoided the trail of foliage. I asked what the significance was to all this ritual, and was informed a funeral was taking place. This was required out of respect for the deceased and served as notice to the greater community. I must say I was impressed.

Later in the drive to our left was an expansive circular bamboo fence. Because we were driving slowly, and being that we were in a remote area, I could hear voices from behind the enclosure. As we got closer to the entry, about a dozen to fifteen or so kids came

Chapter 8: Native People

running to the road and with smiles as wide as the road itself, began waving their arms. Our driver told us they were welcoming us and were happy we had come to visit. As I looked inside the bamboo enclosure, I could see a series of thatched huts. These were their homes, and based upon what I saw in the open space, they had been playing soccer. Having interrupted their game to run to the road and wave to us, displaying enormous smiles, sent a chill up my spine. It was no act, and they weren't expecting anything from us. It was genuinely joy from within their hearts. By the way, the bamboo fencing served as protection from predators. The gates would close at sundown.

One has to respect the simplicity of life here as opposed to the material environment in which we live. People matter to people. They coexist with the most dangerous wildlife on the planet and yet do all they can to protect it. I'm not naive, I'm sure there's conflict from time to time, disagreement, and circumstances that arise that overwhelm them. But if you could see the smiles, hear the laughter, and listen to all the talk amongst them, you'd arrive at a place that's true and very real among people. Ordinary people with very large hearts. I do wonder sometimes if they yearn for more. I'd be surprised to learn that some don't. That said, I've never heard any complain. I owe them a great debt. They have enriched my life tremendously in ways too numerous to list.

One last story. It has to do with my guide, KB, and his tracker. You might recall from an earlier chapter, they guided us in Botswana. They were involved with our elephant encounter at the river, late one afternoon.

Prior to leaving home in April 1998 for our first trip to Africa, I thought there might be a lack of available light in the evening and early morning. In case my assumption was correct, I bought for Tracy, Nichole, and myself inexpensive watches that allowed you to push the stem of the watch in and light the dial. They worked well, and we were glad we had them with us. My assumption had been correct, there was very little available light while in the bush and in camp.

I noticed when out on night drives, every once in a while, one of the girls would light the dial of her watch to see what time it was. It caught the eye of KB and seemed to excite him. In their native tongue, he made the tracker aware of this magic watch. For the remainder of our time in the bush that night, both were fixated on seeing the dial lit up on the watches.

A few days later, we were driven to meet our bush flight to the next camp. While waiting for the plane, because KB had been so accommodating and his tracker so focused on keeping us aware of wildlife activity while on game drives, I asked if there was anything I could send them from the States. Without a half-seconds hesitation,

Chapter 8: Native People

KB said "watches". He even had the mailing address prepared for me. No surprise. I knew that was coming. As soon as we arrived home, I bought two watches and a couple of extra batteries for each and sent them to Botswana. I wasn't convinced they would ever arrive, but they did. Two months later, I received a letter in the mail from someone I didn't know in a neighboring town who had been to that same camp in Botswana sometime after we had departed. I opened the envelope and removed a handwritten note from KB thanking me for the watches. I was stunned. I then researched the sender's phone number and asked how he came about the responsibility to forward the thank you note. He told me somehow KB learned of his being from Massachusetts and asked if he could arrange to forward the note to me. I thanked him for doing so. We then took about fifteen minutes to share experiences while in Africa. Sometimes the things you never expect are the things least forgotten. I was grateful to learn the watches had successfully found their way to KB and his tracker.

I think the people here have been as impressive to me as the wildlife and unending beauty of the landscapes, without question, in a vastly different way. There is a quality about things here that calms you. When I'm here, I don't for one second think about or miss the life I live when I'm home. There's no foolishness here, no pretense, no desire or need to be entertained constantly, I don't sense petty conflict among the people. The simplicity of it all is alluring. I sometimes think I could have done well being born here and living my life in this place that's unquestionably real.

Chapter 9: Observations

I mentioned earlier that from early childhood, I was an extremely observant kid. That trait has followed me throughout my life and will most likely accompany me all the way to my grave. Hopefully, not for quite a while. There's still more Africa to see and just as much golf to play. Possessing that quality has proven to be beneficial to my time in Africa. It's played a valuable part in my understanding of and dealing with the risks involved in being in a place that I can't control to any degree. Wildlife doesn't care who I am, how much money I have, my station in society, who I know, or any other aspect of the species I represent. They, to a degree, tolerate my intrusion but ultimately determine my movement and behavior within this environment. Those who become complacent in the African bush risk great peril. In the case of the incident I'm about to describe, it wasn't my innate ability to observe but rather that of my wife. I'm embarrassed to say I fell asleep on this one.

I've begun this chapter with this statement of fact because of an incident that occurred at a camp in Botswana Judy and I visited in 1999. It was a very intimate camp, located within the Linyanti Reserve, which encompassed the Savuti Channel wildlife region. An area that supported a great number of predators. The camp was very isolated and comprised of only four tents. Our stay would be for four nights. At the time we were there, the channel, which at one time had been a substantial body of water, was now dry and created a clear path for predators to roam. I've been told, in recent years, the water has returned to the channel.

Upon arrival at the camp, we were greeted by a nice young lady who was charged with managing the camp and a few other members of the staff, each kept busy with specific responsibilities. At one point, I noticed my wife assessing the lodge area with a great deal of confusion on her face and looking somewhat concerned. It seemed odd to me being we had never been to this camp and seemingly had no reason to be suspect of anything. Following a brief

Chapter 9: Observations

orientation by the manager, a camp employee brought us to our tent, familiarized us with what we needed to know, and left us to unpack. Judy then commented to me she felt a strong sense that something was very wrong here. I asked why she felt that, and she said she didn't feel the staff was comfortable being at this camp or amongst each other. To her, there was no cohesion and not much warmth among the personnel. She asked if I sensed anything strange, and I told her no, I was simply excited to be there. I could tell from her mood and facial expression this was something she was not about to let go of. Of this I was sure.

While at breakfast the next morning, Judy ate very little and was laser focused on the mood within camp. I knew she hadn't slept well. Following breakfast, we set out on our morning game drive, and throughout the entire time, she was extremely quiet and preoccupied. The morning had been eventful. Wildlife sightings were many, and the landscape simply breathtaking. Still, for Judy, the cloud that seemed to hang over camp would not allow her any sunlight.

When we returned to camp, we walked directly to our tent, and I told Judy she needed to let go of whatever was troubling her. I tried to impress upon her the fact that we'd be leaving in two days and none of what she observed would matter at that point. I don't know why I took the time to say anything. She suggested we walk to the lodge to sit and relax before lunch. We did, and right away she cornered the young camp manager. The two then walked to an area used to look out over the dry channel. They talked for some time and returned with smiles on their faces. I can't begin to tell you how appreciative I was for that. Their conversation seemed to have removed a terrible burden from the mind of the manager. I wish I could remember her name. She seemed to become somewhat more engaging, and Judy appeared satisfied that her observation had been validated. When we returned to our tent after lunch, she told me she had been right all along. Something was wrong, and the reason for it was chilling.

Just prior to our arrival at camp, about a week earlier, a couple was out for a game drive when their guide happened to look out onto the sandy soil and noticed fresh lion tracks. He stopped, made the couple aware of his finding, and proceeded to tell the couple to stay in the car while he walked to pursue what direction the lion had taken. It was not a wise thing to do. To leave guests alone in a Land Rover to follow fresh predator tracks on foot and unarmed, was irresponsible and unwise to say the least. This was a remote area, lion rich and a place wildlife was not accustomed to interaction with people. Not to say they ever truly become accustomed.

Chapter 9: Observations

As the guide pressed on, he lost sight of the lion's tracks. They must have disappeared into a changing soil condition. As he walked by a large bush, a lioness emerged from behind it, jumped the unsuspecting guide, took him to the ground, and began mauling him. Chances are, the lioness perceived him to be a threat. Hearing the screams and growls, the husband of the couple being guided jumped into the driver's seat, started the Land Rover, and drove to where the incident was taking place. He then charged the lion with the vehicle, and she immediately ran to behind the bush from where she had emerged. When she appeared, she was seen walking away with her cub. The perceived threat to her little one was the obvious impetus for the attack. As the guide lay bleeding on the ground, the couple immediately radioed the camp for help. Staff members arrived at the scene and surveying the extent of the injuries, arranged for an air lift as time was of the essence. Unfortunately, too much damage had been done, and survival was impossible. The entire incident was to do with the preservation of the lionesses baby. Wrong place, wrong time, and an unwise decision to walk among fresh tracks.

The shock and horror of such a tragic event created a need to immediately remove the staff and replace them with new people. I have no doubt, left to themselves, any of the staff present at the time would have been willing to remain. I'm sure dealing with the mental images of that horror, those images having originated from that camp, the staff in place at the time would not have been capable of supporting a healthy continuance of service to future guests. My understanding was that there was immediate discussion regarding a search for and putting down of the lioness. Fortunately, cooler heads prevailed, she was rightly spared, and her little one afforded the benefit of being raised by its' mother, as nature intended.

I don't want to seem unsympathetic to this guide's ultimate fate. However, knowing that prior to his licensing to become a safari guide, he was required to be educated as to life in the bush, behavior of the wildlife, and there needed to be a degree of common sense that would work in conjunction with that schooling. In this particular case, realizing his intent was to provide an unforgettable experience for his guests, his judgment was poor. Stopping the car was one thing, exiting the vehicle and deciding to walk and follow fresh tracks of a predator was wrong beyond discussion. It makes me think although the intentions were good, common sense had been left behind. I've said it a thousand times to a thousand people, this is raw Africa. It's not a zoo. Control is governed by the wildlife. Each time I visit, I'm amazed how tolerant they are of my presence. That said, I know they're watching, and if in their mind the need arises, they won't give a second thought to reminding me whose house this is and who governs the landscape.

As a result of the time I've spent on or near rivers in Africa, I've become quite sensitive to and observant of the Nile crocodiles that inhabit these winding bodies of water. They seem to be everywhere. During dry season, I see them lying on exposed sandbars in the middle of the rivers as well as along the shoreline.

They lie perfectly still, reminiscent of lawn ornaments. They're so still, any sign of them breathing is non-evident. Sensing any movement on the river, they quietly and without creating so much as a ripple in the water disappear into the depths, hoping to ambush a meal. If you aren't focused on or see them as you approach, you'll never have the opportunity to appreciate the stealth with which they operate. Sometimes, at a glance, while resting in the shallows of the river, they can appear to be nothing more than a large rock. They've captivated me, and I sometimes sit and watch them for what my guides will tell you is too long a time.

Chapter 9: Observations

Late one morning, while awaiting a wildebeest crossing on a somewhat narrow point on the Mara River in Kenya, my guide and I saw three or four large crocs who were resting on the bank of the river, slide into the water in anticipation of the crossing and the prospect of a chance to capture an early lunch. As soon as the wildebeest entered the water, the crocs began their pursuit. One in particular caught my eye, and I recall paying no attention to all else happening at the moment. At one point, the crocodile I was focused on disappeared below the surface, and shortly thereafter, I observed a lone wildebeest struggling to move forward as if stuck in the mud. The current at this slight bend in the river was a bit strong, and the water level somewhat shallow. It appeared the wildebeest was caught in the current and began an unrecoverable journey downstream. In short order, that was proven not to be the case.

While observing the travels of this one unfortunate animal, I began to hear cries of distress. I asked my guide to drive further along the shore to acquire a closer position to the wildebeest. Suddenly, a splash occurred at the surface of the water, and the croc that had earlier disappeared below the surface emerged and exposed the right rear leg of the antelope firmly in its' jaws. What I believed was the current taking the wildebeest downstream was in fact the crocodile in search of deeper water needed to drown its' catch. My guide, Karia, and I sat for fifty minutes observing the wildebeest struggling to get to shore, where it could gain a footing and hopefully shake off the croc. It struggled mightily and a few times, looked as though it might succeed. Each time the croc surfaced, the wound it had inflicted on the hind quarter of its' prey appeared deeper and considerably more severe, exposing the loss of a considerable volume of blood. The cries were becoming louder and more frequent, and the loss of energy left no doubt as to who would win this struggle. I don't like to admit that I couldn't sit any longer to witness the end, but I was mentally drained, and my eyes told me what they had seen to this point was enough. I don't imagine it was too much longer before the croc took total possession of its' trophy.

Chapter 9: Observations

On a lighter note, sometimes while traversing the expanse of the African landscape on a game drive, you'll have the good fortune to meet and observe the relationship between married couples as they're doing the same. If you allow yourself the temporary luxury of detachment from the seriousness of where you are, funny things will make their presence known regarding these relationships.

One particular day while in Kenya, I remember preparing for an early morning game drive with my guide. The camp chef prepared a fantastic bacon, onion, and cheese omelet for me along with sausage, toast, and an ice-cold glass of orange juice. I could barely lift myself into the Land Cruiser following that twenty-minute exercise. Off we went for the day. I remember not being concerned about seeing or photographing any wildlife. It was strange not to care about that, but I simply wanted to take time this particular day to hopefully see a lighter side of where I was. I thought it might be enlightening to put aside the seriousness of the bush for just one day. Of my many trips to this wonderful place of magic, I never felt what I did this day, totally free and unencumbered. The only responsibility I placed on that day was to me, not the camera or anything else that could be seen as a distraction. I simply wanted to observe all that surrounded me.

Late morning, it happened. The road we were driving along was a typical bush path. It was dirt, somewhat rocky, and in places ladened with long stretches of ruts left by tire tracks of vehicles driven along this road during the rains. Not unusual in these parts. This drive was not for anyone with a bad back. No matter at what speed you're traveling, the tossing around, being bounced up and down, and side to side can be excruciating. Now, I've told you that to tell you this.

It has been my experience that husbands and wives come to Africa for different reasons and expect to experience different things. I think having spoken to many wives, their approach to coming here involves more of an emotional appeal as opposed to their husbands adventurous hopes and expectations. Not in every case, but more often than not. This particular day, I observed something so funny that anytime I feel emotionally down for any reason, I only need to draw on my memory of this short encounter to make me laugh and forget feeling dysphoric.

As we drove along, approaching us from the opposite direction was another safari car with a husband and wife aboard. The husband was seated behind the driver/guide, armed with his camera sporting a lens that appeared to be the length of a baseball bat. His wife was occupying the seat furthest to the rear. Both were dressed quite appropriately, to the extent that their safari garb most likely exceeded the value of the Aston Martin I hope to have before I die.

Chapter 9: Observations

    My opportunity to observe all this came about as a result of my guide knowing theirs. As the cars came side to side, both drivers stopped and, in Swahili, chatted for about five minutes. That gave me a chance to exchange pleasantries with the couple. I could tell from the dismissive posture of the nicely dressed lady she had not much in the way of enthusiasm left for the rest of the day. She had no interest in any conversation. I could tell her tank was near empty. I sensed she had smelled enough elephant dung and been bounced around enough that she was ready for two weeks on the beach. On the other hand, her husband was so energized and excited he wouldn't stop talking and thought it necessary to make me aware of every function available on his camera. I was happy to see he was enjoying himself. I do think he had lost sight of the fact he was going to have to retreat to his tent at the end of the day, with her. The thought crossed my mind, wait until he realizes there's no bus he can put her on to send her to the beach. Is it any wonder why relationships can become so fragile?

    I witness this time and again when I'm in the bush. For some reason, it's so funny to me. It never gets old. I think because I know how much is involved in terms of preparation and resources. In my case, I was very lucky. Judy never complained about a thing. Not once. I know she was uncomfortable every so often while riding in the safari car, but I know she appreciated the experience she was having and was never going to make mine anything but the best.

I realize not everyone who comes to Africa shares my obsession with and passion for this unique place. I also know because travel here is generally arranged in such a way that guests don't usually stay in one camp more than a few days, it can be difficult to focus on anything other than what you see for the moment. Time is limited for most who visit, and you want to see everything in the brief time you have. I get it. Years ago, because I thought I would have only one opportunity to see the African bush, my focus was admittedly quite narrow. As I mentioned earlier, having had the luxury of returning many times and arranging to stay at one camp for longer periods than is common, I've come to greatly appreciate the time to see and observe things beyond the obvious lure of wildlife, not to say that aspect has ever escaped me.

Following a long day of game viewing, dinner is generally served communally at a long table. Conversation among guests usually begins with the exchange of pleasantries and quickly turns to what was seen on the day's game drive. Many times, due to my interests in things beyond the wildlife I see, I sometimes feel left out of the conversation. I understand why I'm not bothered by it. I know I can't engage most at the table in talk beyond the checklist of wildlife they saw, and I feel somewhat sorry they missed a great deal of the true essence of where they are. Through the years, I've had difficulty trying to understand why many of the people who come here don't see beyond the physical presence of what's in their view.

Chapter 9: Observations

I've since come to understand it's up to me to remember, I'm here for reasons they're not, and for whatever reason they came, it will be proven good for them to have done so.

Chapter 10:
In Conclusion

I guess it's time to close. I feel terrible having reached the conclusion of this writing. To this point, seven trips for varying lengths of time over the past twenty-seven years have been exciting, adventurous, enlightening, and beyond overwhelming. I could never have imagined being as fortunate as I've been. My experiences in Africa have been too numerous to include in one short volume. I sense the need could arise at some point to expand upon this current text. There's so much more to tell.

Throughout my life, I've heard many say that someday they want to go here or there, see this or that, or experience something that has captured their imagination at some point in their life. Many factors influence what does or does not allow those ambitions to come to fruition. Some are never serious to begin with. They're just momentary thoughts. Others are quite important, but will be negatively influenced by a lack of resources or not being in a position to allocate the time necessary to realize the dream. Priorities change and require those once important desires to be placed on the back burner. Sometimes, time will run out, and the flame will be permanently extinguished. Often times many of us who must sacrifice and or prioritize in order to achieve a goal, in the end, are

Chapter 10: In conclusion

not seriously willing to do so. Maybe because it really wasn't that important to begin with.

In my particular case, from very early on, Africa was so important many things too numerous to mention had to be set aside. I guess it's all about choices. Just how important is what you desire to see, experience, or have? I've often told people we all have one of two choices to make during our lives. We can choose to exist, or we can make a concerted effort to live our lives. To exist only requires a daily routine of such things as going to work, coming home, mowing the lawn, grocery shopping, and waiting for the obligatory two-week vacation. There generally is no burning desire to expand one's horizons. That's fine. It is, after all, a choice. An oversimplification, maybe, but you get the point. I do understand in some instances, there are circumstances beyond our control that won't permit escape from a life of existence. To live your life requires you to do whatever is necessary to see the places that are meaningful to you, do the things that inspire you, and throughout the process be willing to put aside all else that might get in the way and interrupt the all important pursuit. The rewards for having done so are fulfilling and irrevocable. I can certainly attest to that.

I regret having to put aside some of what I did. I just wasn't willing to sacrifice Africa for places and things I ultimately determined were much less enticing. I will admit there was an element of fear and anxiety to be dealt with in placing so much significance on an African experience. You might recall I spoke to it earlier, the thought while on the plane that I might be visiting no more than a large zoo. At one time in my life, that might have been enough to discourage me. I was extremely fortunate, the fire inside burned too hot and too long to allow that to happen.

Many people have asked what could possibly lure me to Africa time and again. Wildlife doesn't change with time. You see what you saw last time. To some extent, there's truth to that. However, I can assure you no two trips ever provided any semblance of being remotely the same. Each time I visit I see lions, always under different circumstances. I've seen them hunt, I've watched them mate, sleep, and on occasion challenge one another. On the most recent trip, I had the privilege of observing a young male, quite early in the morning, attempt taking possession of a harem from a much older and weaker defender of the pride. The encounter consumed only twenty minutes and was frighteningly nasty and violent. The lionesses could only watch from a distance. When it was over, the old guy had prevailed, but I never had a doubt the young man would return and try again. I knew one day he would succeed. I'd never witnessed a similar confrontation prior to this cool once quiet morning. To date, I've never seen it a second time.

Chapter 10: In conclusion

Speaking of lions, while at another camp two years prior, I sat in the Land Cruiser for approximately thirty-five to forty minutes and watched five female lions tease a lone elderly male buffalo.

They surrounded him and one or two at a time would aggressively charge the old man, forcing him to defend himself while the others would attempt keeping him confined to a small area within the grass. As the lions had done to him, he would charge to fend them off as another lioness staged a mock attack from his backside. As he aggressively spun around to address the attack from the rear, two others approached from his right side. It was all a test to determine how quickly he would tire. It was stunning to watch. All this back and forth was an effort by the lionesses to evaluate the ease or difficulty that would be required to defeat the massive lone bull. In the end, it seemed everyone was exhausted, and the activity ceased. Although he defended himself well, my guide and I agreed nightfall would become his ultimate challenge. Not once during a previous trip had I ever witnessed this game being played. It's just different every time. That's the magic of Africa.

It wasn't until my first venture to Kenya that I saw something I was aware happened quite often, but had never seen. While slowly driving along a path bordering an expansive, open grassy area, my guide and I noticed a female Thompson's gazelle standing motionless just feet off the path we were following. As we approached, she made no effort to escape us and just stared as we drove closer to her. I don't think she was any further than five yards away from the vehicle. As we drove past her I noticed something beginning to protrude from her hind end. I told my guide to stop the car, which he did immediately, at which point we were privileged to witness the birth of a brand new gazelle. In short order, the little one dropped, headfirst from about two to three feet into the grass, whereupon mother immediately began the process of cleaning the newborn, establishing the bond it would need to survive.

Chapter 10: In conclusion

As we sat observing the process taking place, the mother walked away some twenty or thirty yards so as not to bring about unwanted attention to the little one. It was best she wait from a distance for her baby to find its' legs and get to its' feet, something that needed to occur quickly. Upon that happening, she would again unite with her offspring to begin the process of their life in the bush.

My guide suggested we stay to see the little one stand. I told him to move on. I didn't want to be the one responsible for having brought about the unwanted attention of a predator. Living with that thought was intolerable. I suggested we leave the remainder of this magnificent event to nature.

Five previous trips to the bush and thousands of gazelles had never yielded an opportunity to bear witness to an event of this magnitude. Is it any wonder I can't seem to get enough?

No two trips, no two days, and no two encounters have ever been close to the same. This place never stops giving. When it came to Africa, I was not going to let anything or anyone stand in the way of getting there as often as I could. It's a place that has afforded me a unique peace in my life, a greater look into the natural order of things, an appreciation of just how fragile life can be, and the good that comes from being able to generate a smile. I learned a great deal of that virtue from African people. I've said many times, so much in Africa can hurt you. It doesn't matter how large or small it is. However, if you subscribe to the concept of respect and understand your place in the order, you'll be just fine. All that can hurt you here really doesn't want to. Instincts rule their behavior. A word of caution, though, if you come to visit, stay awake. I wish for everyone the discovery of their peace, whenever and wherever it's found.

Thank you for the valuable time you've allocated to reading this text. I hope you've enjoyed doing so. For me, it's been a pleasure to provide. I hope to have more for you in the near future.

I invite you to visit the website at:
theandoniangallery.com

Chapter 10: In conclusion

Please feel free to contact me with any questions you may have or to discuss any content within the book. It excites me to live the experiences over and over again. I welcome it all. It will never get old.

www.ingramcontent.com/pod-product-compliance
Lightning Source LLC
LaVergne TN
LVHW020134080526
838202LV00047B/3935